THE
ORTHODOX
LITURGY

The Development
of the Eucharistic Liturgy
in the Byzantine Rite

Hugh Wybrew

ST VLADIMIR'S SEMINARY PRESS
CRESTWOOD • NEW YORK
2003

LIBRARY OF CONGRESS CATALOGING-IN-PUBLICATION DATA

Wybrew, Hugh.
    The Orthdox Liturgy : the development of the eucharistic liturgy in the
    Byzantine rite / Hugh Wybrew.
        p. cm.
    Includes bibliographical references.
    ISBN 0-88141-100-0
        1. Lord's Supper (Liturgy).   2. Lord's Supper—Orthodox Eastern
    Church.   3. Orthodox Eastern Church—Liturgy.   4. Orthodox Eastern
    Church—Doctrines.   I. Title.
    BX355.W92   1990   90-37967
    264'.019036—dc20   CIP

The Orthodox Liturgy

copyright © 1989 by Hugh Wybrew

First published in the USA in 1990 by

ST VLADIMIR'S SEMINARY PRESS

575 Scarsdale Road, Crestwood, New York, 10707-1699
1-800-204-2665

Reprinted 1996, 2003

ISBN 0-088141-100-0

PRINTED IN THE UNITED STATES OF AMERICA

THE ORTHODOX LITURGY

Other books by
HUGH WYBREW
available from SVS Press

Orthodox Lent, Holy Week and Easter
Orthodox Feasts of Jesus Christ and the Virgin Mary

Contents

Foreword

What is the Church here for? What is the distinctive and unique function of the Church, that which the Church does, and which nobody and nothing else can do? Surely the least incomplete answer is to say: the Church is here to celebrate the Eucharist. The Church is a eucharistic organism, which becomes truly itself when offering the Divine Liturgy.

It is this central action of ecclesial life that the Dean of the Anglican Cathedral in Jerusalem describes in this present book. In a simple and readable manner, he traces step by step the historical development of the eucharistic Liturgy in the Christian East, conveying vividly a sense of what it felt like to worship during each period from apostolic times up to our own day. This is a study based on wide and careful reading, but the results are presented in a manner readily intelligible to the non-specialist. Hugh Wybrew not only describes the words and ritual actions used in the service, but also considers the outer architectural setting with its iconography, as well as the inner symbolism and theology.

The Byzantines spoke of the Church at worship as 'an earthly heaven, in which the heavenly God lives and moves'; and it was precisely this vision of 'heaven on earth' that converted the Russian people to Christianity a thousand years ago. The author conveys with skill the dynamic meaning of the Eucharist for Orthodox Christendom, Greek, Romanian and Slav. Underlying all that he writes there is a deep love for the Liturgy, which he knows well from personal experience. We have long needed such an introduction, clear yet detailed, sympathetic yet not uncritical. This book will be of great value to Christians whether Western or Eastern.

Bishop Kallistos of Diokleia

Preface to the American Edition

This book was originally written for British Christians of Western tradition. It presupposed that their experience of Orthodox worship was likely to be either in Orthodox parishes in Britain or Western Europe, or in the Orthodox Churches of Eastern and South-Eastern Europe or the Middle East. Liturgical practice in these countries is still on the whole conservative, although various modifications to traditional practice have become generally accepted in different places.

It was in these countries that the Orthodox liturgy became a formative part of my own Christian experience. When I was a student I spent a year at the Orthodox Theological Institute of St Sergius in Paris. Subsequently I worshipped regularly with the Russian Orthodox parish in Oxford. For two years, when I was chaplain at the Church of the Resurrection in Bucharest, I often attended Romanian Orthodox services, and was able to share in Bulgarian and Serbian Orthodox worship on my pastoral visits to Sofia and Belgrade. I have come to be as much at home at the Orthodox Liturgy as at an Anglican or Roman Catholic Eucharist – sometimes, in fact, more so. I am grateful to all the Orthodox communities with whom I have worshipped for what I have learnt from them. It is out of these experiences that I written my description of the Liturgy in the first chapter, 'Western Eucharist and Orthodox Liturgy' and from them that I have suggested certain things that Western Christians might usefully learn from Orthodox worship in the 'Epilogue'.

This edition, however, is intended for a North American readership, both Orthodox and non-Orthodox. In North America Orthodox liturgical practice has changed in a number of important respects in recent decades, and the setting in which the Liturgy is celebrated has been modified, too. In most Orthodox churches, of whatever national background, the congregation is provided with pews. Only in more traditionalist Russian parishes, and parishes made up of converts to Orthodoxy zealous for tradition, does the congregation still stand throughout the service. In some newer churches, too, the iconostasis is now open in form, with a wider space in the centre, and often without any doors or curtain. The people can now see what is taking place in the sanctuary and at the altar. In many parishes in all the Orthodox Churches the anaphora is now said out loud, so that the people can associate themselves with the priest in the central prayer of the rite. There is far more congregational participation in singing than in the Churches of Europe or the Middle East. Nearly all Greek parishes have a large mixed choir rather than a single chanter, and the singing is sometimes accompanied by an organ. Frequent communion is now common, not only in parishes of American-born Orthodox, but in many parishes of Greek, Arab, Russian and Romanian origin. The trend toward more frequent communion has, in recent years, spread in Europe, Russia, and the Middle East as well.

Participation in the Liturgy is therefore much more active in North America than in most churches elsewhere, and the contrast between Orthodox and contemporary Western practice is correspondingly less sharp. North American readers should be aware of the difference between what they are used to in church and Orthodox liturgical practice in other parts of the world when reading the first chapter and the Epilogue. But these two sections of the book will still be of use to Christians of all traditions visiting Europe and the Middle East from North America.

I have written the kind of book I should like to have read when I first began to study the Liturgy. It is not at all intended for the expert in either the history of Christian worship or the Orthodox Christian tradition. It is meant for those who have had some experience of the Liturgy, and are curious about its shape and content. It attempts to sketch the history of the Liturgy by describing, at each stage of its development for which there is evidence, what it was like to take part in the Eucharist in the Orthodox East.

Liturgical worship is far more than the use of a form of service. The context in which the words of the rite are used is at least as important as the text itself. That context includes the building in which the service takes place, its furniture and decoration; the ceremonial, or way in which the service is performed; the music to which it is sung; and the understanding of what is done, implicit or explicit in the minds of the worshippers. I have tried to paint a broad picture of each stage of the Liturgy's development including all these aspects. Many details are inevitably missing. They can be pursued in the books to which I owe all that

I know, and from which I have drawn the material from which the picture has been built up. They are listed in the bibliography, and I acknowledge gratefully my debt to their authors.

I am grateful to Bishop Kallistos of Diokleia for contributing a Foreword and for suggesting a number of improvements to the text. I am particularly grateful to Père Michel van Parys and the Benedictine community at Chevetogne in Belgium, who welcomed me so warmly for three and a half months of sabbatical leave from my parish in Pinner, Middlesex, in 1981. I completed my draft there in an ideal setting combining the resources of Benedictine scholarship with Orthodox worship in their Byzantine church. I must also thank my volunteer secretary in Jerusalem, Mrs Mollie Speirs, who patiently and efficiently typed out the text.

The book is dedicated to the late Anne Pennington of Lady Margaret Hall, Oxford, a devoted friend of the Orthodox Church as well as a devout Anglican. Her encouragement prompted its beginnings and inspired its completion.

Hugh Wybrew
Jerusalem, 1989

1 Western Eucharist and Orthodox Liturgy

The Eucharist is celebrated in the Western Churches in a wide variety of ways. Each Christian tradition, Roman Catholic, Anglican or Protestant, has its own distinctive ethos; and within each Church there is a great diversity of style. But a Western Christian familiar with the Eucharist in his own Church will not feel too far from home attending a celebration in another tradition. The movement for liturgical renewal which has led to the revision of forms of eucharistic worship in the Roman Catholic and Anglican Churches and in many of the Protestant Churches has resulted in a remarkable convergence both of forms of service and of manner of celebration. Many differences of detail remain. But all traditions have been influenced by the study of the worship of the Church in the earliest centuries of its life, even if, in all the Churches, some congregations have embraced new forms and new ways with greater enthusiasm than others.

The Western Christian is used to a form of service whose structure is simple and clear. A brief introductory section, often penitential in character, precedes the Ministry of the Word, in which scripture readings and psalms proclaim the Christian gospel. They are more often than not expounded in a homily or sermon. At least on Sundays the Nicene Creed is recited. Then the congregation intercedes for the Church and for the world. The Lord's command to 'do this in remembrance of me' is obeyed in the Ministry of the Sacrament. Bread and wine are brought to the altar and set upon it, and the prayer of thanksgiving, the eucharistic prayer, is recited over them. The Lord's Prayer is said, and nearly all present receive the consecrated bread and wine in Holy Communion. The service ends with a brief conclusion and a dismissal. It is a short service, lasting only about one hour, even when celebrated solemnly with music and singing.

But simplicity rather than solemnity is more often than not the keynote of the modern Western Eucharist. Ceremonial is usually the minimum necessary for the performance of the service. Unnecessary movement or gesture is discouraged, lest the essential structure and movement of the service be obscured. The setting of the service, too, is usually simple. Modern church buildings tend to be simple in their design and restrained in their decoration. It is emphasized that the building is only the place where the living church assembles, and where indeed it may well gather for purposes other than worship. The altar is designed to recall a table, where the Lord's disciples continue to celebrate the meal once eaten by Jesus and the twelve. As a focus of the celebration it must share its prominence with the lectern, from which the Church is nourished by God's Word in Scripture as in sacrament. The use of special vestments is often restricted to the chief celebrant, while readers and others who may be closely involved in the service wear ordinary clothes. Even the priest or minister may on occasion be scarcely distinguishable in dress from the rest of the congregation. In consequence of this fashionable preference for simplicity, it is sometimes hard to distinguish a Roman Catholic celebration from an Anglican or a Protestant.

The active participation of the whole church is a still more prominent characteristic of the modern Western Eucharist. Worshippers are encouraged to join fully in a service which deliberately includes congregational responses to help them to do so. The language of modern rites is simple and straightforward, to satisfy the desire for immediate intelligibility. Members of the congregation are often responsible for the readings and the intercessions, and assist with the distribution of Communion. New churches are designed, and older ones adapted, to associate the people as closely as possible with the altar and those serving at it. The Eucharist must be visible as well as audible, for, even if some distinction still remains between priest and people, it is the whole church which is the active celebrant of the service. Particular importance is attached to participation in the heart of the service, the sharing of the consecrated bread and wine. At a Roman Catholic Eucharist, quite as much as at an Anglican or Protestant celebration, all those present are normally expected to receive holy communion. Participation in the sacrament is not only an integral part of the Eucharist: it is its climax.

Western worshippers accustomed to this form and style of eucharistic worship enter a different world when they go into an Orthodox church to attend a celebration of the Divine Liturgy. They first enter a building whose shape and decoration are not only governed by a tradition going back many centuries, but are considered to have a significance of their own, apart from the rite they have been elaborated to house. Passing through an inner porch, or narthex, they find themselves in a nave, square rather than oblong, devoid of all but a few chairs for the elderly or weak. They look up into a central dome, from whose summit an image of Christ the Almighty looks down majestically on the worshippers below. Round the drum supporting the dome there are prophets and apostles, and a procession of angelic deacons, while on the vaults surrounding the dome, and on the upper portions of the nave walls, are depicted cherubim and seraphim, the four evangelists, and scenes from the life of Christ. Particularly prominent may be those commemorated in the Church's calendar. Lower down are representations of monks and ascetics, martyrs and warriors, bishops and teachers, who enfold the congregation within a pictorial communion of saints.

Behind, on the west wall of the nave, is depicted the Dormition of the Virgin Mary; while to the east rises a screen covered with icons, separating the sanctuary from the nave. It may be comparatively low, or it may reach as high as the roof itself. Pierced by double doors in the centre and single doors to north and south, the icon-screen, in its taller form, largely reproduces the themes of the fresco or mosaic decoration of the nave. To the right of the central, or royal, doors is the image of Christ the Almighty, to the left that of the Mother of God with the Christ-child. On the royal doors themselves is the representation of the Annunciation, while the doors to north and south are adorned with the archangels Michael and Gabriel, or with holy deacons. Immediately above the royal doors there is a representation of the Last Supper. In the second rank of images are the saving events in the life of Christ, commemorated in the great festivals of the Church's year. Above them, in the third rank, are the apostles, turning in an attitude of supplication to an enthroned figure of Christ in the centre, on either side his Mother and St John the Baptist as chief intercessors for mankind. If there is a fourth rank, it contains the prophets, on either side of a Virgin and Child, while the whole screen is surmounted by a cross, bearing a painted image of the crucified Lord – for there are no three-dimensional figures in the church – flanked by the Virgin Mary and St John the Evangelist.

When the royal doors are opened, worshippers see in the middle of the sanctuary, arranged normally within a semi-circular apse, the square altar, richly covered, on which stand a cross, candlesticks, and an ark, often shaped like a church, in

3

which is kept consecrated bread from the Eucharist. They may catch a glimpse of the decoration of the apse. Nearest the ground two rows of bishops, vested for the Liturgy, turn towards the altar. Above them Christ stands at an altar, giving Communion to the apostles, on one side from the consecrated bread, on the other from the chalice. From the semi-dome of the apse, perhaps visible above the icon-screen, the Mother of God looks out above the altar into the nave. But worshippers will almost certainly not see the altar of the prothesis, at which the eucharistic bread and wine are prepared, and to which the north door in the icon-screen gives access; nor will they be able to see its decoration, in which scenes of the birth of Christ may find a place alongside those of his death and burial. Nor can they see into the south apse, which serves as a sacristy and vestry.

So different is the typical Orthodox church, with its many oil lamps and votive candles, and pervasive odour of incense, from the surroundings in which Western worshippers usually pray that they may be less surprised to learn that Orthodox Christians are accustomed to regard the church building itself as a sacrament. Far more than a utilitarian shelter for the congregation, it is an image of heaven on earth. For while the lower portion of the nave signifies the visible world, the dome, and still more the sanctuary, are images of heaven, where the triune God is worshipped by angels and archangels and the whole company of heaven. There Christ offers himself to the Father in an eternal sacrifice of love and self-giving: and into that sacrifice the worshipper is drawn by participating in the Liturgy which celebrates in spiritual reality what the church building proclaims in sacramental image.

Awesome as Western Christians find an Orthodox church, they notice that Orthodox Christians feel more at home in it than they themselves do in their far simpler setting. As the Orthodox come in, they go round the church, and kiss icons, putting lighted candles before them and praying. They may take a small round loaf, called a prosphora, or offering, to the north door in the icon-screen, and hand it in, with a list of names of living and dead, to the deacon or server. There is an atmosphere at once of reverence and of informality, the latter greatly helped by the absence in all save some Greek churches of fixed pews or ordered rows of chairs, such as is rarely found in Western churches, where either the one or the other is normal.

Yet the Divine Liturgy, once it begins, unfolds with a degree of hieratic formality now decreasingly favoured in Western Churches: and does so often with little apparent contribution to its progress from the congregation. Indeed, the first part of the service has been going on for some time before those in the nave become aware that the public Liturgy is about to begin. For perhaps an hour the priest has been performing at the side altar the rite of the prothesis or proskomidia, the preliminary preparation of the eucharistic bread and wine, for which no modern Western rite has any equivalent. But even when the public Liturgy begins, it is performed largely or entirely by the clergy and the singers: for every Liturgy is fully sung, the Western distinction between said and sung celebrations being unknown in the Orthodox Church. Little in Orthodox worship astonishes Western Christians more than the relative silence of the Orthodox congregation. They have been brought up to think that participation in worship means joining in the singing and saying of hymns and prayers. While in some Orthodox churches in recent years the people have come to sing some parts of the service, in others it is still sung by choir or chanters alone.

At the Liturgy, therefore, Western Christians must learn other ways of taking part in the service. It is impossible to attend the Liturgy with the traditional Western 'eyes closed'. Standing throughout the service, except perhaps to kneel at one or two moments, worshippers pray with their eyes: for every movement of the service has its meaning. They pray, too, with their minds, as they follow the chants and the readings. To the prayer of eye and mind they can add the prayer of the body. They may make the sign of the cross frequently, to associate themselves with the progress and the content of the service, and they may bow, with a gentle inclination or a full prostration, as custom indicates. Incense draws their sense of smell into worship, while music touches their emotions. But Western worshippers will not have learnt to participate in these ways before they receive their greatest shock: few, if any, of the congregation respond to the invitation to Communion. What is for them the normal climax of the service may be almost totally missing. Instead, at the very end of the service, they find themselves welcome to join with everyone else in receiving a piece of blessed bread whose name, the antidoron, shows it to be a substitute for the sacrament itself.

If Western Christians have to learn new ways of participating in the service when they attend the Liturgy, they have also to find their way through an order of service which differs significantly

5

from their own. The Liturgy, leaving aside the proskomidia, falls into two parts, the Liturgy of the Catechumens and the Liturgy of the Faithful. They correspond in general with the Ministry of the Word and the Ministry of the Sacrament into which all modern Western eucharistic rites are divided. But although the basic structure of all eucharistic rites is the same in East and West alike, important differences have appeared in the course of their development.

Western worshippers are used to a brief introduction to the main part of the Ministry of the Word. They may be invited to prepare for the celebration by confessing their sins. Having been absolved, they sing the Kyries or the ancient hymn 'Glory be to God on high', or both. A single prayer, or collect, concludes the introduction and introduces the readings. The Liturgy, by contrast, begins with a lengthy sequence of three litanies, one long and two short, each followed by an antiphon composed of a psalm or other chant. The only point of resemblance here with Western rites is the response 'Kyrie eleison' in the litanies, from which in fact the Western Kyries originally derived. After the third antiphon, often the Beatitudes, the clergy emerge from the north door in the icon-screen, bearing the Gospel-book, and, coming into the nave, return into the sanctuary through the royal doors. There follow three kinds of chant: an invitatory, based on the first verse of the Venite, Psalm 95; short hymns prescribed for the day, called troparia and kontakia; and the Trisagion, 'Holy God, holy and strong, holy immortal, have mercy upon us', which Western Christians may have heard sung in their own rite at the Veneration of the Cross on Good Friday. The invitatory bears some family likeness to the psalm verse used as an entrance antiphon or introductory sentence in Western rites: the variable short hymns, though different in form and origin, serve a purpose now not totally dissimilar from that of Western collects. But to the Little Entrance, as the procession of clergy is called, the Western Eucharist contains no obvious parallel.

Not until the Scriptures are read do Western Christians feel themselves on familiar ground. Since the reforms of recent years they are used to three readings: from the Old Testament, the Acts or Epistles, and the Gospels. Between the readings they expect portions of a psalm or a hymn. In the Liturgy they find two readings only, the first always from the New Testament Acts or Epistles, the second from the Gospels. Both are chanted rather than read. Between them psalm verses are sung, with Alleluia as a refrain. They may notice that a few verses of a psalm are sung before the first reading, and wonder whether there was ever an Old Testament reading in the Liturgy. The readings are unlikely to be followed by a homily or sermon. Western worshippers are surprised, and may be relieved, to discover that there is no provision for a sermon to be preached at the Liturgy, though one may be given, most probably at the end of the service, or even, when there are many clergy, during their Communion.

Western visitors now begin to be a little lost. They are not surprised when the Gospel is followed by an intercession in the form of a litany. They are used to the intercession, or prayer of the faithful, coming after the scripture readings and sermon; though they may wonder why the Creed is not recited first, as the congregation's response of faith to the proclamation of God's Word. But they are puzzled when the catechumens are then solemnly dismissed, and no one leaves; and when the faithful are urged to renewed intercession, and given no opportunity to pray. Nothing in their own experience points them to a familiar landmark here. Nor does Western practice provide a reliable guide when, preceded by the first part of the Cherubic Hymn, the bread and wine prepared during the Proskomidia are brought in solemn procession by the clergy out of the north door in the icon-screen, and through the nave into the sanctuary. They may be used to an offertory procession, in which the bread and wine for the Eucharist, and the financial contributions of the people, are brought from the back of the church to the priest at the altar by representatives of the congregation. But in the Great Entrance it is the clergy themselves who bring the elements from one part of the sanctuary to another, and the bread and wine are accorded a reverence which Western worshippers associate only with the consecrated sacrament.

For as the procession appears the people cross themselves and bow, and many may kneel or prostrate themselves as the richly veiled chalice and paten are carried past. In some places they may lay young children in the path of the priest who carries the vessels, so that he steps over them on his way. Meanwhile, the clergy commemorate their church leaders, the rulers of the country, perhaps the sick and those in special need, and the departed, and finally the congregation and all Orthodox believers. Blessing the people with the elements, they take them into the sanctuary through the royal doors and place them on the altar. This, the moment of greatest ceremonial splendour in the

Orthodox Liturgy, is, like the Little Entrance, without parallel in the Western Eucharist.

Unlike the Western offertory procession, the Great Entrance does not immediately precede the eucharistic prayer. It is followed by another litany, and then by the kiss of peace. No sign of peace is given between clergy and people, or among the people, though one is exchanged among the clergy. This might be felt as a lack by Western worshippers, who would in any case be used to the kiss of peace elsewhere: if Anglicans before the offertory and consecration, if Roman Catholics after consecration and before Communion. In the Liturgy it precedes the recitation of the Creed, which serves as the immediate preparation of the eucharistic prayer.

This prayer, called the anaphora, or prayer of offering, is introduced by a dialogue similar to the Western introduction, except that its first greeting is the Grace. Its final response, 'It is meet and right', is lengthier than its Western counterpart. To the surprise of Western Christians, the choir has no sooner sung it than it begins the Sanctus. The first part of the anaphora has been said inaudibly by the priest behind the closed doors of the icon-screen, and he has raised his voice only to give the cue for the Sanctus. The rest of the prayer is said in the same way, punctuated by occasional phrases chanted out loud, to which the choir's response covers the next section of the silent prayer. The only words of significance which the congregation hears are the Lord's words relating to the bread and the cup. Only Roman Catholics who remember the old way of celebrating Mass will recall that until the reforms instituted by the Second Vatican Council the Canon of the Mass was similarly recited *sotto voce* by the priest, while at a Sung Mass the choir performed an elaborate setting of the Sanctus and Benedictus. But to modern Western Christians brought up to regard the eucharistic prayer as the most important part of the service, with which they should fully associate themselves in heart and mind, it is astonishing that it should be said as inaudibly as the priest saying it is invisible. There are places where this traditional practice has been modified in recent years: in some churches the royal doors are left open throughout the Liturgy, and in some part at least of the anaphora is said audibly.

The anaphora is followed by a litany, which first commends the gifts of bread and wine to God, and then repeats the petitions of the litany chanted after the Great Entrance. Then the Lord's

Prayer is sung. The proclamation, 'Holy things for holy people', and its response will be familiar to at least some Anglicans. After the Communion of the clergy, the people are invited to receive. The priest first recites on behalf of any intending communicants a prayer which professes faith, confesses sin, and asks for the fruits of Communion. He gives Communion in both kinds at once by means of a spoon. Western worshippers may be surprised to see babes in arms receiving the sacrament in this way too. Communion over, brief hymns and prayers of praise and thanksgiving bring the Liturgy to its conclusion. The people are blessed, and go up to the priest to kiss the cross used in blessing, and receive the antidoron.

Western worshippers attending the Liturgy for the first time are struck by the many differences, of structure as well as of detail, between the Orthodox service and their own. If they study a complete text of the Liturgy, and enquire how the Orthodox themselves understand the service, two general features will be impressed upon them which are new in their experience of Christian worship.

The first is the way in which, in practice, the Liturgy appears to be two services conducted simultaneously. The one is performed within the sanctuary by the clergy, and is largely both invisible and inaudible to the people in the nave. It consists of the whole of the proskomidia; the prayers accompanying the litanies; a number of other prayers, of which some are the private devotions of the clergy, while others contribute to the shape of the rite itself; and, above all, the anaphora, the most important prayer of the whole service. The other is both audible and visible to the congregation, and is conducted mainly by the deacon, standing in front of the royal doors. It consists of the antiphons and litanies; hymns and chants; readings; the processions of the Little and Great Entrances; the Creed; responses, especially in the anaphora; the Lord's Prayer and Communion; and the final prayers and distribution of the antidoron. The two coincide at some points, such as the readings, the Creed, and the Lord's Prayer, and are interlocked at others: verbally, by the frequent greetings given by the priest from within the sanctuary and by the doxologies chanted out loud at the end of prayers recited inaudibly; visually, by the processions, and frequent appearances of the clergy at the royal doors. Nevertheless, the people in the nave appear, from a Western point of view, to be only passive attendants at the central portion of the service, which takes place behind the icon-screen, while their attention is occupied by secondary chants. The Western Christian cannot help feeling that, while the Liturgy may be celebrated for the people, it is not celebrated by them.

The second characteristic feature of the Liturgy is the way in which nearly all its actions are understood to have a symbolic meaning. This can be seen from the text of the Liturgy itself most clearly in the proskomidia. The bread and wine have to be made ready. But they are prepared in such a way that by what is done and said the incarnation and the passion of Christ are represented. It is less evident in the text of the main part of the service. But when the bread and wine are put on the altar at the end of the Great Entrance, the priest recites some of the hymns of Good Friday and Holy Saturday; and after the clergy have received Communion, they say some of the hymns of Easter Day. Christ's burial is symbolized by the deposition of the gifts on the altar, and his resurrection has been represented by the time of Communion.

If Western Christians enquire further, they learn that these are only the chief moments in an interpretation of the Liturgy which relates every part of it to the earthly life and ministry of Jesus, and which extends its symbolism to the church building and its furniture. The proskomidia represents the incarnation and birth of Christ, and also – because he was born in order to die – his passion and death. The prothesis where it is performed stands for Bethlehem and Nazareth, and also Golgotha. The antiphons at the beginning of the Liturgy represent the time of his hidden life on earth, when he was known only through prophecy. He enters on his public ministry at the Little Entrance, when the Gospel-book symbolizes Christ's first appearance. The Epistle represents the preaching of the apostles, the Gospel that of Christ himself. The Great Entrance symbolizes his last journey to Jerusalem to suffer and die, while the placing of the gifts on the altar represents his burial by Joseph of Arimathea and Nicodemus. The altar is the tomb, the veils over the chalice and paten represent the grave-clothes. The resurrection is symbolized when, after the anaphora, a portion of the consecrated bread is put into the chalice; and when, after Communion, the vessels are removed from the altar and taken to the prothesis, the ascension is represented.

So the whole life of Christ is set before the people every time the Liturgy is celebrated: and if few participate in the service sacramentally, all can do so by contemplating the saving mystery of the incarnation, passion, and glorification of the Lord. Such an understanding of the service seems strange to modern Western Christians, taught to regard sacramental participation in the Eucharist as alone normal. Older Roman Catholics will recall that, before frequent Communion became the rule, they were taught to meditate at Mass on the passion of Christ, every detail of which was symbolized in the movements and prayers of the service. This tradition, which with characteristic variants was common to East and West alike, has died out in the Roman Catholic Church since sacramental participation has been generally restored. It survives in Orthodox interpretations of the Liturgy, at which Communion is still in general rare.

For Western Christians the Liturgy offers an experience of eucharistic worship of a kind which they cannot find in their own tradition, and which for many of them has a profound appeal. Their own rites have been renewed in accordance with what modern scholarship assures them was the practice of the early Church. The Liturgy appears to embody principles widely at variance with those they have come to regard as fundamental in worship: and yet for many of them it provides an experience which is deeply worshipful. Familiarity with the Liturgy provokes at least two questions for the Western Christian: How did a rite which claims to go back to the early Church come to assume a form so different from what we know of early Christian worship? and, Might the Western Churches have something to learn from the eucharistic worship of Orthodoxy? The rest of this book will be largely occupied with answering the first question, but will also suggest some answers to the second.

2 The Sources of the Tradition

The First Century

The Origins of the Eucharist

Writing to the Christians at Corinth in AD 52, St Paul claimed to have received from the Lord the tradition 'that the Lord Jesus on the night when he was betrayed took bread, and when he had given thanks, he broke it, and said, "This is my body which is for you. Do this in remembrance of me." In the same way also the cup, after supper, saying, "This cup is the new covenant in my blood. Do this, as often as you drink it, in remembrance of me"' (1 Cor. 11.23–5).

At the Last Supper, celebrated at the season of Passover, Jesus performed an act of prophetic symbolism. Using the basic elements of human diet he enacted in advance his death on the cross. In so doing he both accepted it and interpreted it. His death was to be an act of willing self-offering to God, and by it a new relationship was to be inaugurated between God and his people. By giving his disciples a share in the bread and the cup, Jesus was giving them a share in all that his death would achieve. From that meal comes the Christian Eucharist. Obedient to the command of Jesus, the Church has 'done this' in order to recall Jesus and proclaim his death until he comes.

For the first few decades of the Church's life, Christians continued to frequent both temple and synagogue. But they also met for their distinctive community act, the Eucharist, which to begin with seems to have taken the same form as the Last Supper: a full, formal Jewish meal. It was clearly so at Corinth when Paul wrote his first letter to the church there. The congregation gathered in the dining-room of one of its members on Saturday evening, the beginning of the first day of the week. It was probably crowded: not everyone could recline at table. Some might have been obliged to sit on the window-sill, like the unfortunate young man at Troas who, having fallen asleep during Paul's lengthy sermon, fell to the ground from the third storey

(Acts 20.9). There were many lights to make the room bright. Everyone had brought their contribution to the common meal. It was not always a seemly performance, as Paul's rebuke to the Corinthians makes clear. Some ate and drank only too well, failing to discern the Lord's Body: by which Paul probably means the presence of the Lord both in the sacrament and in the community, whose poorer members had less than a fair share of the food and drink. 'The cup of blessing which we bless, is it not a participation in the blood of Christ? The bread which we break, is it not a participation in the body of Christ? Because there is one loaf, we who are many are one body, for we all partake of the same loaf' (1 Cor. 10.16–17).

It seems that it was not long after this time that the remembrance of Jesus was separated from the common meal. Perhaps it was to avoid such scandals as Paul had had to rebuke: perhaps it was a matter of sheer practical necessity as the infant churches grew, and a full meal became impracticable. By the end of the first century the remembrance of Jesus was made in bread and wine alone. The resulting service was distinctly brief. It was not long before it came to be attached to the synagogue service of scripture readings, sermon and prayers, which the Christians continued to hold even after they had been expelled from the synagogues of the old covenant. Here was the first radical transformation of Christian eucharistic worship. Eating and drinking still formed its heart: but it was no longer an ordinary meal.

The combined Christian synagogue service and memorial meal came at an early period to be held on Sunday morning rather than Saturday evening. Its two parts broadly correspond with what came later in the East to be known as the Liturgy of the Catechumens and the Liturgy of the Faithful, and with what contemporary Western usage refers to as the Ministry of the Word and the Ministry of the Sacrament. It continued to be held in private houses, in the largest convenient room. But though its setting might be called domestic, its celebration very early came to be properly ordered. Writing at the end of the first century Clement, Bishop of the Church in Rome, speaks in this way of the Eucharist, comparing some of the church's officials with ministers of the sanctuary under the old covenant:

To the high priest (i.e. the bishop) his special liturgies have been appointed, and to the priests (i.e. presbyters) their special place is assigned, and on the Levites (i.e. the deacons) their special services are imposed; the layman is bound by the ordinances of the laity. Let each of you, brethren, make eucharist to God according to his own order, keeping a good conscience and not transgressing the appointed rule of his liturgy' (1 *Clem.* 40, 41).

The Eucharist is an ordered celebration, in which each order in the Christian community has its own proper place and function.

But if it is orderly, it is also corporate. It is impossible to be certain about the precise form and function of the Church's ministry at this time. But it is clear that the bishop, as head of the community, presides at the Eucharist. At about the same time, Ignatius, Bishop of Antioch, speaks of him as representing God himself, while the presbyters represent the apostles, and the deacons Christ. But although clear distinctions within the community exist, it is the whole community which celebrates the Eucharist. In the New Testament there is no order within the Church explicitly referred to as priestly. Christ himself is 'our great high priest' who has offered the sacrifice of himself on the cross, and now eternally presents it in heaven. The whole Church is 'a royal priesthood', called to offer spiritual sacrifices to the God who has reconciled us to himself. Paul indeed speaks of his ministry as an apostle using the language of priesthood and sacrifice. But it will be some time yet before any order in the Church will be explicitly called priestly, and then it will be the bishops. But the comparison between bishop and high priest in Clement of Rome already presages future developments.

The Significance of the Eucharist

Paul says that the memorial which the Lord has given to the Church proclaims his death until he comes. The first generations of Christians eagerly awaited the Lord's coming, and their sense of expectancy was naturally heightened when they gathered for their ritual meal. This sense inevitably weakened as time went by. But for the first generations the earthly meal of the Eucharist was an image of that heavenly banquet in terms of which Jesus had often spoken of the Kingdom of his Father; and when the first complete eucharistic text appears in the East towards the end of the fourth century the Eucharist is seen to be offered by a Church still mindful of the second coming of Christ as well as of his passion and resurrection.

The early Christians, celebrating the Eucharist, looked both forward and backward: backward to the cross, whose memorial they were making, and forward to the second coming, which they eagerly awaited. Yet that does not adequately represent the significance of the Eucharist. The memorial, or anamnesis, of Christ made with bread and cup was less a looking back to a past event than a making present of that event here and now. The early Eucharist was no memorial service for the dead founder of the community. When thanks were given over bread and cup, and when the community ate and drank, the crucified and risen Christ was invisibly among them, present no longer in the flesh but in the Spirit. Had he not said, 'Where two or three are gathered in my name, there am I in the midst of them' (Matt. 18.20), and, 'Lo, I am with you always, to the close of the age' (Matt. 28.20)? Nor was the second coming a remote future event. Christ was not absent from them, he was present with them; and where he was, there was the Kingdom of God. The Eucharist was a foretaste of that Kingdom.

For the Christ who was present as the invisible celebrant of the rite, and who gave himself to the participants as the bread which came down from heaven, was himself in heaven. Eternally he presented the sacrifice which was himself at the heavenly altar. It was not inappropriate that when St John the Divine described the vision of the worship of heaven which he saw when he was in the Spirit on the Lord's Day he did so in terms of the Sunday worship of the congregation on Patmos. On the bishop's chair, covered with a white cloth, God was seated, before him the golden altar, around him the presbyters in their appointed place, transformed into heavenly elders. In the midst was the Lamb, standing as it had been slain. Before the throne stood the congregation, the multitude which no man can number. The praise of the elders echoed that of the Church below: for they praised God for creation, for redemption, and for having made them kings and priests to himself – the themes of the thanksgiving said over the bread and wine by the middle of the second century – while the four living creatures sang the Sanctus of Isaiah, praising God with their 'Holy, holy, holy'. For if the Eucharist looks back to the Last Supper and the cross and forward to the final consummation of God's purpose, it also looks upward to the realm where the cross is an eternal reality, and where the Kingdom is not a future hope but a present joy. St John, describing the worship of heaven in terms of the Sunday

Eucharist, can claim to be the forerunner of many a Byzantine preacher and liturgical commentator, explaining the earthly liturgy as an image of the worship of heaven, whereby men and angels join in the common praise of their creator and redeemer. The Eucharist in the first century was a simple rite with a profound meaning which could be grasped only by those who had been initiated into it. Its significance was to a large extent expressed by the prayer of thanksgiving said over the bread and wine. Modelled on the Jewish berakah, or prayer of blessing, such as Jesus used at the Last Supper, it gave thanks for God's mighty work in the creation and salvation of mankind. We have no clear idea of the contents of the prayer at this time, though perhaps the Revelation of John reflects its main themes. But the meaning of the service was not exhausted by the content of the prayer, and never has been. The Church has always seen more in the Eucharist than could be expressed in one prayer. St Paul, as we have seen, attached deep significance to the breaking and sharing of the one loaf: if the Eucharist is a means of communion with the living Christ, it is also an expression of the unity of his Body the Church. Paul may have been the first, but was by no means the last, to see symbolic meaning in the actions of the Eucharist beyond the primary meaning of the rite as the commemoration of the passion and resurrection of Christ. We should notice too the importance Paul gave to what was to be called the kiss of peace, which at the end of several of his letters he exhorts the congregation to exchange. Destined to become a normal part of Christian worship, and to be included in the fully-developed eucharistic liturgy, it was an expression of that spiritual love, or agape, which ought to bind Christians to one another within the love of God.

The New Testament interprets the death of Jesus in terms of Old Testament sacrifices. The Last Supper was held in the shadow of the paschal sacrifice of the unblemished lamb. Christians came quite naturally to speak of Jesus as the Lamb of God. The passion and resurrection constituted a new and greater Passover, by which mankind was freed from slavery to sin and admitted into the Promised Land of the glorious liberty of the children of God. The sacrificial atmosphere of the Last Supper was naturally and inevitably inherited by its ordained imitation, the Eucharist, which celebrated the accomplished sacrifice of Christ on the cross. It was of course true that in fulfilling the sacrifices of the old Law Jesus had totally transformed the

17

meaning of the sacrifice: for what gave the offering of his body and blood on the cross its value and power was not the material offering, but the obedience inspired by love which it embodied. The Christians' response to this sacrifice offered on their behalf was itself described in the New Testament as a sacrifice. 'Present your bodies as a living sacrifice', says Paul (Rom. 12.1). 'Through him then let us continually offer up a sacrifice of praise to God', urges the Epistle to the Hebrews (13.15). The 'spiritual sacrifices acceptable to God' which Christians are enjoined to offer (1 Peter 2.5) and which consist in nothing less than a life consumed by love for God and the brethren, may or may not have been explicitly focused on the Eucharist in New Testament times. But it is clear, when evidence has become available, that the Church regarded the Eucharist as the sacrifice of the New Covenant, in which her own responsive self-offering to God, made in the power of the Holy Spirit, was taken into the sacrificial self-offering of her Lord. That sacrifice, offered once for all on the cross, was eternally presented in the heavenly tabernacle, and continually represented in the Church's commemoration of it in the Eucharist.

The Second and Third Centuries

The Eucharistic Rite

The first description of the Eucharist that we have comes from the *First Apology* of Justin, a native of Asia Minor who became a Christian teacher at Rome, and a martyr. Writing in defence of Christians about AD 160, Justin describes both the Sunday Eucharist, and the Eucharist which followed baptism. In the latter case, the synagogue service seems to have been replaced by the rite of initiation.

The Sunday Eucharist consisted of readings from the Scriptures, sermon, and intercessory prayer, perhaps concluded by the kiss of peace, which was certainly given at the end of baptism before the Eucharist began. This was clearly the Christian form of the Jewish synagogue service. Then bread and wine mixed with water were brought to the president of the brethren. Justin, writing to convince the emperor of the harmlessness of Christians, avoids technical Christian terms: but the president was no doubt the bishop. The president then gives thanks over the bread and wine according to his ability: there were no fixed texts for the eucharistic prayer at this time. But there were traditional themes which he followed. They were thanksgiving for creation, for redemption through the cross, and for our having been accounted worthy of these things. We should not be far wrong in supposing this to be a reference to the royal priesthood of the Church, in virtue of which Christians celebrate the eucharistic sacrifice. This at any rate is the equivalent theme of thanksgiving in the *Apostolic Tradition* of Hippolytus of Rome early in the third century.

The thanksgiving concluded, the bread is broken, and all present share in the bread and wine. It was unthinkable that anyone should be present without communicating. Indeed, so vital was regular communion considered that deacons took some of the bread and wine to those unable to be present: to slaves on duty, or perhaps even to those in prison for their faith in Christ.

This service is characterized by thanksgiving, in Greek *eucharistia*. Not only does the solitary prayer consist, apparently, largely of thanksgiving, but the bread and wine over which thanks have been given are themselves called *eucharistia*. Hippolytus, a little later, spoke of the bread and wine being 'thanked' – 'eucharistized' – into the 'type' of the Body and Blood of Christ. But by the thanksgiving and the thankoffering of the bread and the cup the memorial of the passion of Christ is effected. Although Irenaeus of Lyons, at the end of the second century, emphasized the Eucharist as a thankoffering of the first-fruits of creation, the view that came to predominate was that of Cyprian, that the sacrifice offered in the rite was the passion of Christ.

The Church was clear, too, that what was received in Communion was not ordinary food and drink. The bread and wine which had received the thanksgiving, or the invocation of God, were the Body and Blood of Christ, spiritual and heavenly food.

The early Church had not yet worked out a theology of consecration. Thanksgiving played an important part in the prayer. But it is probable that from an early time the bread and wine were explicitly offered to God in memory of the passion, and that God was asked to accept them at the heavenly altar. The old Latin Canon of the Mass expressed a very ancient concept of the Eucharist when in the prayers after the narrative of institution it offered to God the bread of eternal life and the cup of everlasting salvation in memory of the passion, death and resurrection of Christ, and asked that they might be taken by God's angel – probably Christ himself – to the altar on high. Confident that

God would accept what she offered at Christ's express command, the Church could receive back her gifts as God's gift of the Body and Blood of Christ. From the second century great importance came to be attached to the words of Christ himself in the narrative of institution, which came to form part of almost every later eucharistic prayer.

The Eucharist at this period was celebrated by the whole Church, or, as we might more truly say, by Christ himself acting in and through the whole of his churchly body. Each order concelebrated with the others in its own way. The bread and wine for the sacrifice were brought by the people. They were dealt with by the deacons, who prepared sufficient for the service before the eucharistic prayer, and distributed the consecrated bread and wine at Communion. The bishop as the presiding member of the community, the father of the family, uttered the prayer of thanksgiving in the name of the whole Church. Round him at the altar were the presbyters, the council of elders who assisted him in the government of the church.

The People's Gifts of Bread and Wine

One small but significant variation in practice must be noted here. The people, both in East and West, brought the bread and wine for the Eucharist to church with them. What did they do with them? When the evidence becomes clear, a divergence between Western and Eastern practice has become established. In the West, they brought their gifts to the chancel barrier after the readings, sermon and prayers, where they were collected by the deacons. Sufficient were then set aside and placed on the altar for the Eucharist itself. But it seems that in the East they handed in their offerings on their way into church, either at a table near the door, or in a small room specially provided near the entrance. A mid-third-century document from Syria, the *Didascalia Apostolorum*, prescribes: 'But of the deacons, let one stand always by the oblations of the Eucharist: and let another stand without by the door and observe them that come in; and afterwards, when you offer, let them minister together in the church' (*Didascalia*, ed. Connolly, p. 120).

This apparently unimportant variation in church custom was to have enormous significance in the development of the Byzantine Liturgy. For after the Ministry of the Word the deacons carried to the altar such of the bread and wine as was needed for consecration and Communion. While in the third century, and for two centuries more in Constantinople, this was a purely practical action effected in silence and without ceremony, it was to become in time the most splendid moment of the whole Liturgy, dignified with as much pomp as the Church could muster, and invested with such significance that it became the focal point of popular devotion.

The Setting of the Eucharist

Meanwhile, in the third century, the Church continued to meet in private houses: flats in large apartment blocks in Rome and the big cities, small houses built around a small central courtyard elsewhere. The Church was still illegal and could not own property corporately. Nevertheless in the course of the third century Christians in some places were building themselves special meeting halls. That in Nikomedia was so large and impressive that it provoked complaints from non-Christian citizens. More frequently the Christian community acquired a house, in the name perhaps of its bishop or one of its members, and adapted it for its various needs: social, charitable, educational, and liturgical. Such a house-church was acquired by the congregation in Dura-Europos in Mesopotamia around 231. One

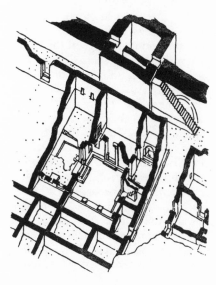

Christian community house at Dura-Europos (Salhiyeh) in Mesopotamia. Built soon after 200, it was later converted for use by the Christian community. On the left is a large meeting-room, made out of two original rooms, probably used for the Eucharist. On the right is the baptistry.

0   60 FEET

0   20 METRES

21

room was turned into a baptistry, while two others were run together to provide a room large enough for a eucharistic gathering of some fifty or sixty people. At its east end was a dais for the bishop. Although the baptistry was decorated with frescoes, the main room was plain.

Even if worship took place in a domestic setting, it was not necessarily lacking in a certain splendour. Paul, Bishop of Samosata in the sixties of the third century, had a lofty throne erected on a dais in the meeting-hall. Attached to it was an audience chamber. When he entered the room for services he was acclaimed by the congregation like a Roman magistrate. Paul's pretensions were thoroughly disapproved of by his episcopal brothers, though, as it turned out, he was only anticipating the shape of things to come. The congregation at Cirta, a small town in North Africa, met in an ordinary house. But it possessed a rich collection of gold and silver vessels, and bronze lamps and candlesticks. Despite occasional persecutions the Church was growing rapidly in strength throughout the third century, laying the foundation for its remarkable expansion in the next.

The Birth of Iconography

From the third century comes the first evidence of Christian iconography. The house-church at Dura contains the earliest frescoes known in a Christian building, while earlier in the century frescoes were used to decorate the catacombs in Rome used for Christian burial. The catacomb paintings make use of themes appropriate to funerary art. The conventional image of the Good Shepherd, an expression of philanthropy, represents Christ. The figure standing with arms raised in prayer, known as the orant, represents the pious soul. Christ and the apostles were shown as fishermen: and a fish was the recognized early Christian symbol for Christ himself, since the Greek word for fish, *ichthys*, was spelled by the initial letters of the phrase, Jesus Christ Son of God and Saviour (*Iesous Christos Theou Yiou Soter*). Sometimes the sacraments of baptism and the Eucharist were depicted, often in a rather allusive manner. Certain scenes from Old and New Testament Scriptures are found: Jonah and the whale, Daniel in the lions' den, Noah and the ark, Abraham and Isaac, the raising of Lazarus, and the adoration of the Magi. The latter was shorthand for the whole of the incarnation and redemption, and counterbalanced the representation of Adam and Eve, standing for the state of sin from which we need deliverance. Most of the scenes depict the salvation of individuals in response to their faith and prayer, and correspond to the prayers made for the dead: in the past God has saved these individuals, may he now save those who have died. Other images are less easy to interpret. There recurs the conventional image of the mother and child. But it is not clear whether this always represents Mary and the child Jesus.

The iconography of the catacombs arose in a liturgical setting, that of prayer for the dead. The frescoes at Dura also relate to the liturgy, this time of baptism. Behind the font, which is placed beneath an arched canopy, are Adam and Eve, and, much larger, the Good Shepherd and his flock. They symbolize original sin and the redemption wrought by Christ. The surviving frescoes include the Samaritan woman at the well, Christ walking on the water, the raising of Lazarus, and the resurrection of Christ, shown by means of the three women at the tomb. The healing of the paralytic is there, and so is David's victory over Goliath. These all point to the victory over evil and the new life and health which baptism confers.

There are no instances known from the third century of Christian decoration of the eucharistic hall. But the images found in the catacombs and at Dura make it clear that the iconography which was later to play so important a part in the decoration of Christian churches, especially in the Byzantine tradition, had its roots in the Hellenistic art of the third century, adapted to express fundamental Christian themes.

One other aspect of late classical art was to become of great importance in the Eastern Christian tradition, both in private devotion and in corporate worship, and that was portraiture. It is quite probable that Christians began painting portraits of distinguished and venerated members of the Church very early on. The Apocryphal Acts of John tell of a portrait of the Apostle which one of his disciples, Lycomedes, commissioned from an artist friend. Lycomedes put it in his bedroom, and adorned it with flowers. John is said to have disapproved. But Lycomedes found it perfectly natural to venerate the portrait of one who had become his spiritual benefactor. The fourth-century historian Eusebius tells of a statue said to be that of Christ which existed in Palestine, and did not think it strange. He had heard too of portraits of Peter and Paul.

Till the fourth century portraits of Christ were rare. The earliest representations seem to have been of the apostles, especially of Peter and Paul, though Christ was shown in scenes from the Gospels. Towards the end of the third century there appeared a kind of collective portrait of Christ seated among the apostles, an image based on a common classical form depicting the teacher and his disciples, or a group of learned men gathered round their leader.

There is little doubt that Christians followed contemporary practice in having funerary portraits painted of distinguished church members. These portraits showed the bust of the person, facing forward, often enclosed within a medallion. There may have been some reserve on the part of the church leaders towards these images in the early centuries, for fear of idolatry. But when the pagan ancestor cult was declared illegal at the beginning of the fifth century such portraits of the saints survived to become the main source of the portable icon. Well before that, and perhaps as early as the third century, Christian images were venerated by being garlanded with flowers and having lights burnt in front of them.

The Interpretation of the Eucharist

To the third century, if not earlier, may be traced the roots of that symbolic interpretation of the Liturgy which was to become an integral part of the Byzantine and Orthodox tradition. The third-century Alexandrian theologian Origen, building upon an earlier tradition, developed a theology of the Christian mystery which profoundly influenced subsequent Eastern theology. The mystery is the reality of salvation, made present in a visible sign which both reveals and conceals it. Origen applies this sacramental principle to the whole of the Christian economy. Christ himself is the fundamental Christian mystery, in whom God and man are united, so that the divinity is both concealed by the humanity, yet revealed by it to those who have eyes to see. Those who have faith see the humanity, but believe in the God who indwells it.

The mystery who is Christ is presented to us in the Scriptures, the Church, and the sacraments. In all three the literal, outward and apparent reality conceals an inner spiritual reality. We must learn to see in the letter of Scripture the spirit, in the Christian community the incarnate Word, and in her visible rites and ceremonies the saving activity of God. So the eucharistic banquet is a symbol of the union of the soul with the divine Word of God, and prefigures the perfect union to which we look forward at the end of time. But the different aspects of the rite also have symbolic value, as well as the whole. The altar, for instance, is the symbol of our interior worship: the smoke of the incense represents the prayers offered by a pure conscience. The bishop is the symbol of Jesus, the priests are Abraham, Isaac, Jacob, and the apostles: the deacons are the seven archangels of God. Bowing the knee symbolizes inner humility and obedience: the kiss of peace expresses genuine love. For Origen the Christian rite fulfils its prefigurations in the Old Testament, expresses the spiritual worship we are meant to offer now, and is the image and anticipation of the worship of heaven. But all this requires that those taking part in the rite be initiated into its true significance, which does not lie on the surface.

Origen's teaching about the Christian mystery and the Liturgy as one means by which it may be apprehended is the soil from which grew one strand in the Byzantine tradition of liturgical interpretation and initiation. Developed by Dionysius the Areopagite in the fifth century and Maximus the Confessor in the seventh, it was taken up and given its final form in the fifteenth century by Symeon of Thessalonike.

3 The Fourth Century

Doctrine and Worship

In 313 Constantine issued the edict of tolerance which transformed the situation of Christians in the Roman Empire. From now on the Church was under imperial patronage, and in the East Constantine, though not baptized until the end of his life, came to be venerated as equal of the apostles. Representations of the Emperor, and of his mother Helena, together with the cross she found in Jerusalem, are often found in the decorative scheme of later Byzantine churches. Favoured by Constantine at the beginning of the century, Christianity became the official religion of the Empire towards its end, under Theodosius I.

Imperial patronage had immediate and profound consequences for the Church, not least in its worship. The Emperor's influence soon made itself felt, even in the domain of doctrine. The fourth century was one of fierce doctrinal conflicts within the Church. Early in the century the Alexandrian presbyter Arius raised a storm that was to rage for half a century and disturb Christendom for far longer by teaching that the Son was not God as the Father was God, but was a creature, albeit the first and highest of all created beings. A good deal of early Christian writing did imply the subordination of the Son to the Father. But once the explicit affirmation of his inferiority had been made, it was seen to strike at the heart of Christian faith in salvation through Christ. If it was not God who was in Christ, reconciling the world to himself, then we are not saved. While the Arians rallied round appropriate slogans such as 'There was when he (the Son) was not', the defenders of what was to be defined as orthodox doctrine were led by Athanasius, Bishop of Alexandria, who adopted the term *'homoousios'*, 'of one substance', as the formula best suited to describe the relationship of the Son to the Father and to defend biblical faith in philosophical terms.

The Emperor could not allow the Church which he intended to be a unifying force within the Empire to be riven by doctrinal disputes. He convoked a Council of all the bishops of the Empire at Nicaea in 325 and presided over its deliberations. Arius was condemned, and Christ pronounced to be 'of one substance' with the Father.

But the argument went on, and in the reaction against the adoption of the novel, non-biblical term *homoousios* the Arians seemed likely to win the day. Not until the 360s did it become clear that the Nicene party would succeed in their defence of the decision of 325. By then fresh disputes were raging over the status of the Holy Spirit, whom extreme Arians were treating as a created being, subordinate to both Father and Son. It was the three Cappadocian fathers, Basil the Great, his brother Gregory of Nyssa, and Gregory of Nazianzus, whose trinitarian teaching was approved at the Council of Constantinople in 381, clearly defining orthodox Christian belief. God is one *ousia*, or 'substance', and three *hypostaseis*, or 'persons': the Father is God, the Son is God, and the Holy Spirit is God: yet there are not three Gods, but one God. It was an affirmation of faith demanded by the biblical revelation and the Christian experience of God.

These trinitarian disputes left their permanent mark on Eastern worship, particularly in the doxologies with which liturgical prayers concluded. The early Christian tradition had been to pray to the Father, through the Son, and in the Holy Spirit. But this tradition had been cited by the Arians in support of their teaching that the Son was subordinate to the Father. 'Glory be to the Father, and to the Son, and to the Holy Spirit' became the appropriate doxology to express and safeguard orthodox doctrine. 'To you we ascribe glory, to the Father and to the Son and to the Holy Spirit, now and for ever and to the ages of ages' became the characteristic ending of Byzantine liturgical prayers, even when, as in the case of the Lord's Prayer, it was not appropriate. For the God to whom the Church continued to pray corporately in the Liturgy was God the Father, as the eucharistic prayer and other older prayers made clear.

The Rise of Constantinople

In 330 Constantine transferred his capital to the small town of Byzantium. Situated on the European shore of the Bosphorus and occupying an easily defended position, it was the ideal site for the capital of an Empire which extended from Scotland to Egypt, from North Africa to the Danube, from the Atlantic to Mesopotamia. Renamed Constantinople, the New Rome was rapidly rebuilt on a scale suited to its function, and its bishop, from being a suffragan of the see of Heraklea, became overnight one of the most important bishops in the whole Church. The Second Ecumenical Council of 381 recognized the see of New Rome as second after that of Old Rome; and by the middle of the fifth century it had as its proper diocese Asia Minor, Thrace, and the coastal areas to the north of the Black Sea.

By the fourth century certain important Churches had come to be centres of liturgical influence for their surrounding neighbours. Rome, Alexandria and Antioch were already well established. Jerusalem rose to rapid prominence as a result of the keen interest shown in the Holy Land and its Christian sites by the imperial family. Byzantium had been within the ecclesiastical province of Antioch, whence it derived its eucharistic liturgy either directly or by way of Pontus and Cappadocia. In the fourth and fifth centuries the links between Constantinople and Antioch were further strengthened by the translation of several bishops of Antioch to the capital. But the New Rome naturally became itself a centre of ecclesiastical and liturgical influence, and the rite of the Great Church of the Holy Wisdom, begun by Constantine and completed only after his death, gradually spread further afield, to become by the end of the twelfth century virtually the only rite of the Orthodox Churches.

The Setting of the Liturgy

If Christians had already shown a tendency to erect buildings of impressive size for their worship, the Peace of the Church enabled a rapid and remarkable growth in the number and magnificence of the churches built all over the Empire. For those built in its capitals and leading cities, and for those which rose over the holy places in Palestine, the imperial treasury was open, and all the resources of architects, masons and artists available.

The design most often followed was that of the basilica, a large rectangular hall. Usually it had side aisles separated from the central space by rows of columns, and an apse at one end. Such halls were used for a variety of purposes, and they were well enough suited to the needs of the Church's worship in the new era. So characteristic were they that the Latin word *basilica* gave the Romanian language the word *biserica*, meaning both church building and Christian community. They could accommodate easily the rapidly swelling congregations, which in the big cities might number many thousands. They provided, in the apse,

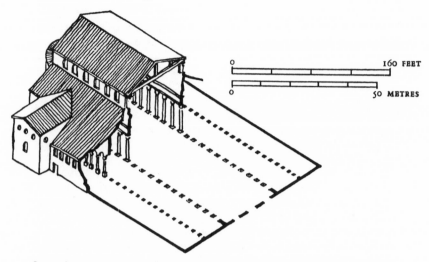

Isometric reconstruction of the Lateran Basilica, the cathedral of Rome, as in 320.

suitably dignified seating for the bishop, who rapidly acquired the status of senior imperial official. Surrounded by his presbyters, he presided over liturgical gatherings as a magistrate over the lawcourts. Within the apse, or some way in front of it, stood the holy table, and the whole space of the sanctuary was protected from the crowds by chancel barriers: waist- or chest-high stone slabs supported by low pillars, such as protected the Emperor or magistrates in similar situations. The people gathered in the nave and aisles, which were often of vast proportions, and adorned with marble columns and marble sheathing on the walls and pillars. The lavish use of marble was complemented by mosaic decoration. If the exterior appearance of such churches was plain, the interior was impressively rich, and designedly so: for the Church was the Church of the Empire, and must worship accordingly.

Imperial Influence on Iconography

Curiously, there seems to have been no immediate flourishing of Christian iconography after the Edict of Toleration. The first initiatives came from the imperial palace rather than from the leaders of the Church. Constantius had the monogram of Christ, the Chi-Rho symbol, placed on military standards and helmets, so putting the army and the state under divine protection. Using a formula employed in antiquity for depicting gods, the Emperor caused representations of himself to be put on coins and medals. He was shown seated on a throne in majesty, while from above the hand of God came towards him, blessing or crowning him. This image expressed the Byzantine theology of empire: the earthly state was a reflection of the divine Kingdom, and its emperor ruled by divine authority as the earthly image of the Lord of the Universe.

The palace art of the fourth century exercised a decisive influence on the development of Christian iconography. It was the model for representations of Christ enthroned as ruler of the universe, surrounded by angels and saints. As the emperor enthroned gave to the high officials of the empire the scroll containing their authorization, so Christ gave the new Law to Peter. Such images expressive of the power of Christ were often placed in the semi-dome of the apse in basilican churches.

From imperial art too came that rigidity of expression and immobility which characterized much later Christian representation. They were held to be essential characteristics of the emperor and his officials, elevated as they were above ordinary human weakness and aided by divine grace. Martyrs came to be shown wearing court dress, a cloak fastened on the shoulder by a clasp, and with a tablion, the square of material denoting honourable rank, at their side. Christ presided over the assembly of the apostles as the emperor presided over a council in the Sacred Palace. He sat enthroned with them at the last judgement as the tribunal sat in the law courts. Even such scenes as the adoration of the Magi and the entry into Jerusalem betrayed the influence of imperial iconography in their manner of representation: the Magi offered gifts to Christ as princes might offer presents to the emperor in a triumph, and Christ entered the holy city as the emperor might enter a captured town.

The style of official imperial portraits, too, contributed to the formation of Christian iconographic portraiture. Neither were portraits in the strict sense. They showed their subjects in such a way as to make clear his or her official status. The portrait of an emperor was precisely that, rather than the portrait of an individual who held the imperial office. Christian iconographic portraiture did, it is true, come to attribute certain consistent

31

features to individual saints: but in the nature of the case these were not true portraits, but variations on a particular manner of representing official people. Following antique custom, such portraits were often enclosed within a circular medallion.

In art as in architecture imperial patronage made an important contribution to the formation of the Christian tradition. In the fourth century it seems to have influenced the choice of themes as well as their manner of presentation. But the stylistic influence remained even when later the Church took the initiative in developing fresh themes.

The Development of the Hierarchy

The Church had from the beginning been a structured society, although there had been a relatively short period – roughly till the end of the first century – when there was a variety of ministries, some local and some itinerant. The bishops had inherited at least some of the functions of the apostles in the government of the local church, in which they were assisted by the presbyterate. Only gradually did the presbyters acquire sacramental functions, as the Church spread, and they were required to look after separate congregations that sprang up within the territory of the bishop's diocese. In his sacramental and liturgical functions the bishop was assisted by the deacons, who often had responsibility for the charitable work of the local church.

We have already seen Paul of Samosata arrogating to himself the trappings of secular dignity. With the public recognition of the Church in the fourth century all the bishops found themselves enjoying the status of senior imperial officials. They soon came to be preceded, like their elder colleagues, by lights and incense when they made their official way to church. Like them, too, they wore the dress of the Roman upper classes, made obligatory for imperial officials by Theodosius I. Over the linea, the undergarment, they wore the tunica, and on top of that the casula. These garments developed into the alb or sticharion, the deacon's tunicle, and the chasuble or phelonion. But in the fourth century the clergy were indistinguishable in their dress from any decently attired Roman official. They certainly wore their best clothes when they presided over the Christian assembly: and some took to wearing a pallium, as a badge of office, and even a girdle, in origin part of military as distinct from civil dress.

But many bishops were opposed for a while to the display of

outward marks of dignity. Celestine I, Bishop of Rome in the early fifth century, insisted that it was by holiness rather than special adornment that bishops should be distinguished. Yet although the development of ecclesiastical vestments was still in the future, clothes of special quality were coming to be thought appropriate for use in church in the fourth century. Constantine is said to have given a 'splendid garment' for use in Jerusalem, and towards the end of the century the *Apostolic Constitutions* directs the bishop to put on a splendid vestment before beginning the eucharistic prayer.

But civil preferment was not the only factor which enhanced the status of the bishop at this time. By the fourth century the bishop was commonly called the high priest, and presbyters priests. A growing tendency to think of Christianity in Old Testament terms further encouraged a distinction between priesthood and people. Under the Old Covenant only the High Priest could enter the Holy of Holies: so, under the New, only the priests could enter the sanctuary to minister at the altar. The royal priesthood of the whole people of God faded before the growing priestly splendour of bishop and presbyter. They were invested with a holiness denied those who had not been ordained. The chancel barriers which protected the new Christian magistrate in his apse also served to separate the ordinary members of the church from those permitted to enter the new Christian holy of holies, the sanctuary. This distinction was reinforced by new developments in eucharistic theology and piety.

Eucharistic Theology and Piety

About the middle of the fourth century Cyril of Jerusalem, or perhaps, later, his successor, John, composed the catechetical lectures given to those preparing for baptism. The last five lectures were delivered after the candidates had been baptized, chrismated, and had taken part for the first time in the Eucharist. They explained the significance of the rites of initiation through which the newly-baptized had recently passed. The fourth and fifth of these *Mystagogical Catecheses* deal with the Eucharist. They are the first evidence we possess of fourth-century eucharistic theology and devotion, and they reveal several characteristics significantly different from what we know from previous centuries. From Cyril's description of the rite in mid-fourth-century Jerusalem it emerges that the Eucharist was quite definitely regarded as a sacrifice. But it was less a sacrifice of thanksgiving than one of propitiation. The eucharistic prayer seems to have consisted of a thanksgiving for creation concluded by the Sanctus, in which the Church on earth is united with the heavenly hosts above. Cyril describes what follows in these words:

> Then having sanctified ourselves by these spiritual hymns, we call upon the merciful God to send forth his Holy Spirit upon the gifts lying before him: that he may make the bread the Body of Christ, and the wine the Blood of Christ, for whatever the Holy Spirit has touched is sanctified and changed. Then after the spiritual sacrifice is perfected, the bloodless service upon that sacrifice of propitiation, we entreat God for the common peace of the Church, for the tranquillity of the world, for kings, for soldiers and allies, for the sick, for the afflicted; and in a word for all who stand in need of succour we all supplicate and offer this sacrifice. Then we commemorate also those who have fallen asleep before us, first patriarchs, prophets, apostles, martyrs, that at their prayers and intervention God would receive our petition. Afterwards also on behalf of the holy fathers and bishops who have fallen asleep before us, and in a word of all who in past years have fallen asleep among us, believing that it will be a very great advantage to the souls, for whom the supplication is put up, while that holy and most awful sacrifice is presented (*Mystagogical Catechesis* 5.7, 8, 9).

On the face of it, the eucharistic prayer described by Cyril consists of a brief thanksgiving for creation, an invocation of the Holy Spirit, or epiclesis, on the gifts, and a lengthy and comprehensive intercession. To some historians of Christian worship such a prayer, containing no institution narrative and no thanksgiving for redemption, has seemed so improbable that they have supposed Cyril to be mentioning only the salient features of the prayer. However that may be, what is significant for the development of eucharistic theology and piety is that he mentions only what he does. The chief interest of the mid-fourth-century Church in Jerusalem was in offering a propitiatory sacrifice that would do good to those for whom the prayer was made in as close association as possible with the sacrifice. Several features of Cyril's description of the service must be noticed.

First, there is a new way of speaking of the presence of Christ in the Eucharist. The Church of the first three centuries was clear that Christ was present at its celebration, as the active invisible

The Passionist Missionaries
526 Monastery Place
Union City, New Jersey 07087-3398

George Vida

celebrant. For Cyril he is present rather as the passive victim. Christians in the early centuries did not doubt that in Communion they received the Body and Blood of Christ, the bread of eternal life and the cup of everlasting salvation. But Cyril speaks of the consecration of the elements as bringing about a change of an almost chemical kind: he cites the changing of water into wine at Cana in Galilee as an example of the kind of change effected in the Eucharist. The East anticipated the medieval Western doctrine of the real presence by many hundreds of years.

This change is brought about by the Holy Spirit. Cyril here reflects the fully-developed theology of the Third Person of the Trinity which emerged in the fourth century in the course of theological argument and was proclaimed as the orthodox doctrine of the Church in 381 at the Council of Constantinople. Cyril is quite clear that 'whatsoever the Holy Spirit touches is sanctified and changed'. In the Eucharist this doctrine received expression in the invocation, or epiclesis, of the Holy Spirit in the eucharistic prayer. Cyril is the first witness to this fully-developed epiclesis which became characteristic of Eastern eucharistic prayers. The West, by contrast, did not adopt the new fashion, and the eucharistic prayer of the Roman Mass continued to pray for consecration in an older way, by asking God to accept the gifts at his heavenly altar. Nicholas Cabasilas, in the fourteenth century, was to point to the Roman prayer as equivalent in function to the Eastern epiclesis: but it reflected an older and rather different view of the Eucharist. This older view was not lost from the Byzantine Liturgy: it continued to be expressed in the litany after the eucharistic prayer and elsewhere.

If the epiclesis in Cyril's prayer reflects a new theology of consecration, the intercession expresses a new understanding of the purpose of consecration. The Holy Spirit is invoked to change the bread and wine into the Body and Blood of Christ so that in the presence of the divine victim the Church may intercede for herself and the world, the living and the dead. It is significant that Cyril can speak of the sacrifice as accomplished as soon as the epiclesis has been uttered: Communion is no longer essential to the rite. The intercession had previously followed the Ministry of the Word. There may have been a certain element of petition in the earlier eucharistic prayer, as there was in the Jewish blessing. But a comprehensive intercession was certainly a new departure in the fourth century, and owed its inclusion in the prayer to the new emphasis on propitiation. It must be noticed how in this view of the Eucharist the theology of the New Testament is reversed. St Paul speaks for the whole of the New Testament in affirming that God was in Christ reconciling the world to himself. But in Cyril's teaching it is not we who are reconciled with God, but God who is propitiated by the sacrifice of Christ which we offer, and is so inclined to hear our supplications. It is significant that from the fourth century the eucharistic prayer is called in the East the anaphora, the prayer which offers the sacrifice. The West called its prayer the canon: short for *canon gratiarum actionis*, the fixed way of giving thanks. But in neither East nor West was thanksgiving the dominant note it had been in the second and third centuries.

The new development in the understanding of consecration found expression in the people's devotional use of the sacrament. Cyril's description of Communion is revealing:

> Approaching therefore come not with your wrists extended or your fingers open: but make your left hand as if a throne for your right, which is on the eve of receiving the king. And having hallowed your palm, receive the Body of Christ, saying after it, Amen. Then after you have with carefulness hallowed your eyes by the touch of the holy Body, partake thereof, giving heed lest you lose any of it; for what you lose is a loss to you as it were from one of your own members. For tell me, if any one gave you gold dust, would you not with all precaution keep it fast, being on your guard against losing any of it, and suffering loss? How much more cautiously then will you observe that not a crumb falls from you of what is more precious than gold and precious stones? Then, after having partaken of the Body of Christ, approach also to the cup of his Blood; not stretching forth your hands, but bending and saying in the way of worship and reverence, Amen, be hallowed by partaking also of the Blood of Christ. And while the moisture is still upon your lips, touching it with your hands, hallow both your eyes and brow and other senses. Then wait for the prayer, and give thanks unto God, who has accounted you worthy of so great mysteries (*Mystagogical Catachesis* 5.21, 22).

These recommended communion devotions imply a holiness attaching to the consecrated elements that is almost physical in nature: the mere touch of the sacrament has power to sanctify. But if it is an almost material holiness, it is also a holiness which is terrifying. The word used by Cyril and usually translated 'awful' means literally 'that which makes the hair stand on end'. The Eucharist is terrifying: only 'having sanctified ourselves by these spiritual hymns' can we proceed to call on God to send his Holy Spirit to change the bread and wine. This testifies to a significant change in the way the Eucharist is understood. St Paul had emphasized how awesome it was to receive the sacrament, and how necessary was proper preparation. But Cyril used the language of awe and fear for the sacrament in itself: merely to be in its presence is cause for fear and trembling. No wonder that the celebration of the mysteries became more and more the preserve of the priests, whom ordination enabled to invoke the Spirit and stand in the presence of the sacrifice. The laity could only behold in reverence and fear.

The differentiation of clergy from laity was still further emphasized by the decline in lay participation in the sacrament which began in the latter part of the fourth century. St Ambrose, in his catechetical lectures to the newly baptized in Milan, probably in the 380s, urged them not to imitate the Greeks, who received the sacrament only once a year. Perhaps the many conversions to the new religion of the Empire somewhat cooled the fervour of the average Christian, although admission to the Church still required a thorough testing and preparation of candidates for initiation. But the new teaching of Cyril and the growth of the ascetic movement combined to discourage frequent communion. Preparation for communion, it was urged, should include abstinence from sexual intercourse: one aspect of the increasing reversion within the Church of the New Covenant to the ritual holiness demanded under the Old. Cyril points to the showbread of the Old Testament as a prefiguration of the bread of the Eucharist: and that could only be eaten by those whose 'vessels were holy' (1 Samuel 21.4, 5). The result of such tendencies was to keep the laity away from communion except on rare occasions. In the conservative West frequent communion survived for several centuries more. In the East lay communion went into a decline from which it has scarcely begun to recover.

The trend in eucharistic theology and piety reflected in Cyril of Jerusalem profoundly affected the worship of the Byzantine Church. The whole-hearted enthusiasm with which Jerusalem seems to have adopted new ideas and practices may not have been fully shared by other churches. But the liturgical practice of Jerusalem and the theology which it expressed were absorbed into the Eastern tradition, making a prominent contribution to its development. The language of fear with regard to the sacrament appears again in the teaching of St John Chrysostom, and is reflected in the Byzantine Liturgy: while the characteristic features of the eucharistic prayer in Jerusalem appear in the first Eastern eucharistic rite which has survived, that of the *Apostolic Constitutions*.

The Liturgy of the Eighth Book of the *Apostolic Constitutions*

The *Apostolic Constitutions* is a handbook of church teaching and practice dating from the last quarter of the fourth century. Based on earlier works of a similar kind, it claims to be the ordinance of the apostles transmitted to the Church by Clement of Rome. The Liturgy contained in the eighth book is therefore often called the Clementine Liturgy. The earliest complete text of a eucharistic rite to have survived, it represents in general the usage of the Church of Antioch, although it was perhaps never actually used. The compiler of the book was somewhat unorthodox, though not positively Arian. For the history of Christian worship its character as a specimen rite has great value, for unlike those rites which have been used it has not been modified to accord with developing practice. In its general form it can be taken as representing the rite of Antioch in the late fourth century, from which that of Constantinople ultimately derived.

The number of resemblances it contains to the developed Byzantine Liturgy, whose first surviving text dates only from the end of the eighth century or the beginning of the ninth, is striking; and it is worth while looking closely, in order to have an impression of the shape of the Eucharist at Constantinople at the beginning of its independent development as the rite of the Eastern capital. Within the scheme of the *Apostolic Constitutions* the Clementine Liturgy is that celebrated by a newly-consecrated bishop.

The congregation gathered in a church that was pointed towards the east, rectangular in shape, and with sacristies on either side at the east. The people were carefully segregated, men on one side, women on the other. The elderly had seats, the younger people too, if there was room. Children had to be kept in order by their parents. It was the task of the deacons to make sure that people went to their proper place and behaved themselves.

The Liturgy began after the bishop's enthronement with

scripture readings. The rubric speaks of the Law, the Prophets, the Epistles, the Acts and the Gospels. It is not clear whether passages from each were read on every occasion. In a summary description of the Eucharist in the second book the reader is said to stand on some high place in the midst: no doubt an ambo, or pulpitum, placed in the centre of the nave. The second book also mentions the Psalms of David, which from an early time were sung in between the readings, and specifies that the Gospel should be read by a deacon or presbyter. After the readings came the sermon, or sermons. The Clementine Liturgy says that the bishop preaches after he has greeted the church with the Grace. The second book indicates that he preached last, after the presbyters had had their turn. He preached sitting, from his throne, the symbol of his teaching authority as well as of his government of the Church.

There followed the dismissal of all those groups not entitled to take part in the Eucharist itself. The Clementine Liturgy reflects the fourth-century organization of the Church, which, in addition to those who were baptized and communicant members, included catechumens being prepared for baptism, energumens believed to be possessed by unclean spirits, illuminati in the final stages of preparation for initiation, and penitents excluded from communion while they did penance for grave sins. Each of these groups was dismissed in a similar way. They were bidden to pray by the deacon, while he led the faithful in a litany of supplication for them. After the prayers of the church on their behalf they rose from their knees and bowed their heads while the bishop prayed over them. The deacon then dismissed them.

When only the faithful were left they were invited again to pray, this time in a comprehensive litany for the whole Church. To each petition in this and every other litany in the rite the people responded, Kyrie eleison, Lord have mercy. The litany was concluded by a prayer for the people said by the bishop. This form of corporate prayer was to become characteristic of the Byzantine rite. It appears first in the fourth century. An older way of making corporate intercession survived in the Roman rite in the Solemn Prayers of Good Friday. There the people were bidden to pray for a particular category of persons. The deacon instructed them to kneel and silent prayer was made. He then gave the command to arise, and the priest recited a short collect, in which the silent prayers of the faithful were gathered together. This ancient way of praying left its traces in other rites too. They may even be detected in some of the petitions of the Litany of the Faithful in the Clementine Liturgy, which have a composite form: they begin 'Let us pray for . . .' and continue 'that the Lord may . . .' These two parts may represent respectively the bidding and the concluding prayer of the ancient form: the silent prayer has disappeared, the two parts have coalesced to form one petition, and the people, instead of praying in silence, shout out Kyrie eleison at its conclusion. In origin this seems to have been a non-Christian exclamation, similar to the old English 'God bless my soul!'

After the prayers of the faithful the bishop greeted the church: The peace of God be with you all. The people replied: And with your spirit. The kiss of peace was then exchanged. By this time the kiss had come to be linked with the Eucharist itself, rather than with the end of the Ministry of the Word. Cyril of Jerusalem mentions it immediately before the eucharistic prayer, and explains its meaning by referring to Matthew 5.23: 'If you bring your gift to the altar, and there remember that your brother has something against you, leave your gift before the altar and go your way, first be reconciled to your brother, and then come and offer your gift'. But the mutual charity and reconciliation symbolized by the kiss of peace was strictly controlled by the Clementine Liturgy and subsequent practice: the clergy saluted the bishop, the laymen the laymen, and the women the women.

Preparations were then made for the celebration of the sacrament. The rubric in the Clementine Liturgy provides an interesting insight into some aspects of fourth-century worship:

> Let the children stand near the bema (sanctuary) and let one of the deacons preside over them so that they be not disorderly. And let other deacons walk about and observe the men and the women, so that there may be no disturbance, and that none may nod or whisper or sleep. And let the deacons stand at the men's door, and the subdeacons at the women's door, so that none may go out, and the door may not be opened, not even by the faithful, during the time of the anaphora.

Meanwhile one of the subdeacons provides the priests with the means of washing their hands. The lavabo is first mentioned by Cyril, though before the kiss of peace. It was one of the earliest symbolic additions to the service. Jews customarily washed their hands before prayer, and Christians seem to have continued the practice: fountains were often provided at the entrance to churches. But this lavabo seems to be a specifically clerical rite. Both Cyril and the Clementine Liturgy say it symbolizes the spiritual purity which should characterize the priests ministering at the altar.

The deacon then again dismisses those not entitled to remain: perhaps as a final precaution, since they should already have left. He summons the faithful to draw near, bids mothers take charge of their children, warns those in uncharity or hypocrisy and concludes: 'Let us with fear and trembling stand upright before the Lord to offer.'

The deacons then bring the gifts to the bishop at the altar. There is no mention of where they come from or how they were provided. But it is probable that the people had brought bread and wine to church with them, and had left them, perhaps in one of the two sacristies which flanked the east end of the building. It has been observed that the deacon's admonitions would come more logically after the bringing in of the bread and wine. But liturgy is not always logical: though it is quite possible that the compiler of the *Apostolic Constitutions* has here put his sources together clumsily.

The rubric preceding the anaphora sets the scene for the eucharistic prayer:

> And let the priests stand on his (the bishop's) right and on his left, as disciples standing by a teacher. But let two deacons on either side of the altar hold a fan of thin tissue or of peacock's feathers, and let them gently ward off the small flying creatures, so that they may not approach the cups.

The presbyters still have their proper place as the real Clement of Rome described it at the end of the first century:

> Then let the high priest (the bishop), after praying by himself together with the priests, and putting on a splendid vestment, and standing at the altar, and making the sign of the cross with his hand upon his forehead say: 'The grace of the Almighty God, and the love of our Lord Jesus Christ, and the communion of the Holy Spirit, be with you all.'

In the fourth century all the prayers of the Liturgy were public prayers. It was no doubt natural for the clergy to pray in preparation for the Eucharist: but their prayer was silent and informal. St Paul's prayer at the end of his Second Epistle to the Corinthians became the characteristic introduction to Eastern anaphoras. In the Clementine Liturgy it was followed by the exhortation: 'Lift up your minds' and the response: 'We lift them up to the Lord'; and the injunction: 'Let us give thanks to the Lord', with the people's reply: 'It is meet and right'.

The anaphora of the Clementine Liturgy is of great length and could hardly have been composed for use. But its structure is of great interest. It begins with an extended thanksgiving to God for his own being, and for the creation which he brought into being through his only-begotten Son. A detailed description of the natural order based on Genesis 1 and 2 is followed by an equally detailed account of God's work in redemption up to the collapse of the walls of Jericho. Here the thanksgiving breaks off to conclude with a mention of all the hosts of heaven, leading into the Sanctus.

The prayer continues with praise for God's holiness, and that of his Son, and with a thanksgiving for the work of the incarnate Christ as far as his ascension. It then moves on to the formal commemoration of the passion and the offering of the gifts: 'Wherefore we, having in remembrance the things which he for our sakes endured, give thanks to you, O God Almighty, not such as are due but such as we can, and fulfil his injunction.' The account of the institution at the Last Supper follows. Then, 'Therefore having in remembrance his passion and death and resurrection and his return into heaven, and his future second advent in which he shall come to judge the quick and the dead, and to give to every man according to his works, we offer unto you our King and our God, according to his injunction, this bread and this cup, giving thanks unto you through him that you have counted us worthy to stand before you and to sacrifice unto you'. God is asked to look graciously on the gifts lying before him and to be well pleased with them. For this part of the prayer the compiler of the *Apostolic Constitutions* drew upon the early third-century *Apostolic Tradition* of Hippolytus of Rome.

Up to this point the prayer, eccentric though it be in the detailed nature of its thanksgiving for creation, represents the understanding of the Eucharist which seems to have predominated in the first three centuries. In the verbal thanksgiving of the Church for creation, redemption, and its own royal priesthood is enfolded the thank-offering of the bread and wine in accordance with Christ's command.

But in what follows the influence of the newer tradition first seen in Cyril of Jerusalem is dominant. For the anaphora goes on to ask God to 'send down upon this sacrifice your Holy Spirit, the witness of the sufferings of the Lord Jesus, that he may declare (or make) this bread the Body of your Christ, and this cup the Blood of your Christ, that they who partake thereof may be strengthened in godliness, may receive remission of their sins, may be filled with the Holy Spirit, may become worthy of your Christ, and may obtain eternal life, you being reconciled unto them, O Master Almighty'.

There follows a comprehensive intercession for the Church and the episcopate, for the celebrant himself and all the clergy, for the emperor and the civil and military authorities, for the departed, the congregation present, the city, persecutors, the catechumens, energumens and penitents, for seasonable weather and the fruits of the earth, and for those reasonably absent. The whole anaphora concludes with a trinitarian doxology and the Amen of the people.

If the first part of the prayer reflects the traditional emphasis of the Eucharist in offering the sacrifice of praise, the latter part reflects the newer interest of the fourth century in offering a propitiatory sacrifice. In the Clementine Liturgy the newer tradition has already been combined with the older, and the resulting pattern of the eucharistic prayer became that of all subsequent Eastern anaphoras.

The bishop greeted the people with: 'The peace of God be with you all', and the deacon proclaimed a series of petitions, which summed up the contents of the intercession in the anaphora. But the first is of special interest: 'Let us pray for the gift which is offered to the Lord God, that the good God may, through the mediation of his Christ, receive it upon his heavenly altar for a sweet-smelling savour.' It is in substance the same petition made in the old Latin Canon of the Mass in the paragraph beginning 'Supplices te'. Reflecting an older theology of consecration, it is curiously juxtaposed with the newer theology of consecration by the invocation of the Holy Spirit. It soon came to be understood as a petition for the acceptance of the consecrated gifts, rather than as a petition for consecration.

The older and newer concepts of the Eucharist, which both contributed to the shape of the Eastern anaphora, continued to coexist in Byzantine eucharistic theology. Theologians spoke of Christ, now as the invisible celebrant of the Liturgy, offering the sacrifice of all the Church, now as the passive victim offered by the Church to God in order to propitiate him. The later prayer of the Great Entrance combined them verbally when it said of Christ: 'For it is you who offer and are offered.'

The litany after the anaphora ends with the bishop's prayer for worthy Communion of clergy and people. The Lord's Prayer was not said. It was introduced into the Eucharist as a preparation for Communion in the course of the fourth century. Although it was in the rite of Jerusalem when Cyril gave his catechetical lectures, it had evidently not yet been adopted in Antioch. By the early fifth century St Augustine could say that it was used in practically every church.

After the litany the deacon called out: 'Let us attend'. The bishop invited the people to Communion with the words: 'The holy things for the holy people'. This too first appears in the Jerusalem rite. The people's response began with the 'There is one holy, one Lord Jesus Christ, to the glory of God the Father' familiar in the later Byzantine rite, but went on to elaborate it.

Communion was given to the clergy and people in due order with the words 'The Body of Christ' and 'The Blood of Christ', to which the communicant said 'Amen'. During Communion Psalm 33 was said. After Communion any of the remaining consecrated gifts were taken to the sacristy. The deacon invited the people to thank God for having been granted to participate in the holy mysteries, and the bishop gave thanks in the name of all, in a prayer which was also a general supplication. The deacon then instructed the people to bow their heads, while the bishop prayed for them, so giving them God's blessing. They were then dismissed by the deacon.

The Clementine Liturgy enables us to form a reasonably accurate picture of late fourth-century eucharistic worship in the province of Antioch. It testifies to the consolidation of the liturgical tradition in the East, parallel to that revealed by Ambrose of Milan in the West. The eucharistic prayer, which at least up to the third century had been extempore, at the discretion of the bishop, now became a fixed text. There was of course nothing like the uniformity of text and practice which later came to characterize eucharistic worship throughout the Church. It was still possible for new eucharistic prayers to be composed, of course following traditional lines; and considerable variety existed in the manner of celebrating the service. But the Clementine Liturgy provides us with a reasonable guide to the basic shape of the Liturgy of Constantinople at the end of the fourth century, as well as containing a number of features which are closely paralleled in the rite of the capital when clear evidence for its form and details appears. It offers us an adequate starting-point for tracing the specific development of Byzantine eucharistic worship.

4 The Eucharist at Constantinople in the time of John Chrysostom

John the 'golden-mouthed' won his reputation as a preacher during his years as a priest at Antioch, 386–98. In the latter years he was chosen unwillingly to be Bishop of Constantinople. For six years he presided over the church in the capital, endeavouring to reform its life and morals. The hostility of the Empress Eudoxia and of Theophilus of Alexandria caused him to be deposed in 404, and he died in exile three years later. In his own day he was associated with liturgical reform, and Byzantine and later Orthodox tradition came to link his name inseparably with one of the two eucharistic rites of the Byzantine Church. From his sermons preached in the capital we can form some impression of the Eucharist there in his time, while scattered literary references and the results of archaeological investigations enable us to place the Liturgy in its architectural setting.

The Churches of Constantinople

Chrysostom no doubt officiated in each of the several large churches with which the city had been adorned since 330. In addition to the original Hagia Sophia, the Great Church begun by Constantine and completed by Constantius in 360, which served as the cathedral, there existed the High Church, Hagia Irene, close by, and the Church of the Apostles, the former enlarged and beautified by Constantine, the latter built by him.

These churches were all basilicas, and although none has survived, we can be reasonably certain of their chief features. Worshippers entered first through an imposing portico, whose doorway might be hung with rich curtains. They found themselves in an atrium, or forecourt, surrounded on three sides by a columned arcade. In the middle was a fountain where the faithful could wash their hands on their way into church, as much in

47

preparation for prayer as for receiving the sacrament. The atrium was also where the poor gathered in the hope of receiving alms from the churchgoers.

The church itself was entered by way of the narthex, or porch, on the fourth side of the atrium. Several doors led into the narthex, where people could gather before the service began. Whether or not they entered the church before the bishop arrived is not clear. Certainly in the first half of the seventh century the congregation seems to have gathered outside the church, and to have entered it only after the bishop had made his ceremonial entrance. The larger churches of the city all seem to have had doors at the east end, on either side of the apse, as well as at the west end, and often in the north and south sides too. The central doors leading from the narthex into the nave were known as the royal doors, and it was through them that the Emperor entered with the Patriarch into the church on those occasions when he took part formally in the Liturgy.

The nave was rectangular, and might have two or four side aisles, separated from the central part of the church by rows of columns. Usually there were galleries above the aisles, and above the narthex too. Access to these was by way of a stair or ramp approached usually from outside the church. The churches of Constantinople were characterized by a sense of openness. The aisles were not separated from the nave by barriers, nor, as has sometimes been supposed, by curtains. Men and women were separated in church, the women occupying the north side, the men the south. It has often been held that the women used the galleries, but it seems more probable that, although they might do so, they were not excluded from the nave or aisles. Later, if not in Chrysostom's time, space was reserved in the gallery for the Empress and her suite, and sometimes the Emperor took part in the Liturgy from his special place in the gallery.

From the seventh century at any rate the gallery was commonly called the catechumenon. Perhaps this points to one of its principal uses. It is not clear whether or not the catechumens and other special groups distinguished from the main body of believers had a place of their own assigned to them in church. It would certainly have been appropriate for the catechumens, unable to receive Communion, to have been in the gallery which was cut off from the nave once the outside doors of the church had been closed. In Chrysostom's time the catechumenate was still a living institution. As it declined and finally, after the seventh century, disappeared, the gallery was put to other uses. Oratories for private prayer were made there, and later they contained a variety of rooms for imperial use. From time to time efforts were made to prevent lovers making profane use of them.

At the east end of the basilica the sanctuary, the place for the bishop and his clergy, occupied the semicircular apse and sometimes extended into the front part of the nave. It was enclosed by a low chancel barrier. There was an entrance in the middle, and usually, if the sanctuary extended beyond the chord of the apse, on the north and south sides too. The short pillars supporting the chancel slabs might be surmounted by small columns, on which rested an architrave, a decorative beam. There is no reason to suppose that in Constantinople this screen was not left open, so that the congregation had a clear view of the sanctuary. Within it stood the altar table, of stone or precious metal, and with rich coverings. It was often enhanced by a ciborium above it, a dome resting on four columns, made of stone or precious metal. Again, there seems no good reason to think that the altar was at any time during the Liturgy screened from view by curtains hung between the columns of the ciborium, although this may have been the case elsewhere, and has often been thought to have been so in Constantinople. Beneath the altar, in at least two fifth-century churches, there was a small vault for relics, to which a flight of steps gave access immediately behind the altar.

Behind the altar rose the bishop's throne, set against the wall of the apse. On either side ran the bench for the clergy. In Constantinople it was at the top of a number of steps, so that the bishop could both see and be seen above the altar. It was from his throne, or cathedra, in the apse that the bishop usually preached, seated, although Chrysostom often preached from the ambo in the middle of the nave, in order to be better heard.

In the churches of the city the ambo stood roughly in the middle of the nave. It consisted of a raised platform enclosed with a parapet of stone slabs, to which two flights of steps gave access. It was connected with the sanctuary by a protected way called the solea: a narrow passage bordered by stone slabs set into pillars in the same way as the sanctuary barrier. It might connect immediately with the sanctuary, or there might be a gap between the two. In either case the solea enabled unhindered passage through a crowded church between sanctuary and ambo.

The Celebration of the Eucharist

It was in this setting that Chrysostom presided over the celebration of the Eucharist. He entered with his attendant clergy through the central, royal, doors leading from the narthex into the nave. He was preceded by lights and incense, and by a deacon carrying the book of the Gospels. When the procession reached the sanctuary the Gospels were placed on the altar as a symbol of Christ, the Word of God, and the clergy went to their respective places. The bishop gave the greeting: 'Peace be with you all', to which the people responded: 'And with your spirit'. He then ascended the throne for the readings. From Chrysostom's sermons it is clear that there was often a great deal of noise in the church at the beginning of the service, and it might take some time before anything like silence was achieved.

The bishop's greeting was the signal for the scripture readings to begin. They were three in number, and were read from the ambo. A deacon first called out: 'Let us attend', an appeal that was by no means a formality. The reader announced the book from which the prophetic reading was taken and began: 'Thus says the Lord'. The second reading was taken from an Epistle, and was presumably preceded by a similar call for silence. For the Gospel everyone stood: presumably during the first two readings those who could sat or squatted. Chrysostom implies that a reader also read the Gospel, although elsewhere it was becoming the custom that the Gospel, as the most important of the readings, should be read by a deacon or priest. Later it was normally read in Constantinople too by a deacon, except on Easter Day, when it was read by the bishop himself. It is probable that between the readings a responsorial psalm was sung, with a refrain sung by the congregation between the verses.

In several of his sermons Chrysostom reproached his congregation for their lack of attention during the readings. People, it seems, complained that there was no point in listening, the readings were always the same. He reminded them that it is God himself who speaks to us through the prophet and the apostle, and still more through the Gospel.

He seems to have had no such problem with his homily or sermon. In fact he reproached those who saw no point in coming to church unless there was to be a sermon. In practice there were often several sermons at the Eucharist at this time. Even though Chrysostom himself occasionally preached for two hours, his sermon came sometimes after that of one or more bishops or priests. He always preached last as the senior bishop. The homily was preceded by the bishop's greeting, 'Peace be with you all', and its response. It was usually delivered from the throne in the apse, the bishop seated, the people standing. When Chrysostom preached from the ambo, a chair was no doubt placed for him there. The custom of preaching or teaching from a chair was in all probability continued from Jewish practice in the synagogue. Jesus is said to have sat down to teach, and early Christian art showed him seated in the midst of his disciples, teaching. In the early Church continuity of apostolic teaching from the same chair was an important aspect of apostolic succession.

Not even a preacher of Chrysostom's eloquence was always heard attentively. He had cause to complain of those who cracked jokes and laughed during the sermon, and did not stop laughing even when the prayers began. On the other hand his sermons, like those of other popular preachers, were often interrupted by applause. The prayers took the form of litanies of the kind we have noticed in the Clementine Liturgy. In all probability the catechumens were first prayed for and dismissed, and then the penitents. The latter certainly formed a recognizable group in the Church, for Chrysostom remarked that people were often more ashamed of being recognized as sinners than of having committed the sin itself. When the catechumens were dismissed, Chrysostom noted with disapproval that some of the faithful seized the opportunity to leave with them, so refusing to take their part in the mysteries that were about to begin. There is no evidence as to whether or not those classified as possessed by unclean spirits formed a distinct group at Constantinople for whom prayer was made at the Eucharist before they were dismissed. Once those groups whom ecclesiastical discipline did not permit to take part in the Eucharist itself had left, the faithful were again called to prayer on their knees. Biddings were included for the empire, for the Church spread out to the ends of the earth, for peace, and for those in any kind of trouble. Probably these themes, enumerated by Chrysostom, were amplified in a larger number of biddings, to which the people responded: Kyrie eleison. Chrysostom stressed the greater efficacy of corporate prayer by comparison with individual, and insisted that in intercessory prayer the whole Church was united: there was here no distinction between clergy and laity. He may well have found it expedient to underline a unity which was already being undermined by church architecture, liturgical and devotional practices, and even theology.

It was now time for the bread and wine to be brought in for the Eucharist. In preparation for this the bishop once more greeted the people: 'Peace be with you all'. When they had made the usual response the deacon exhorted them to 'Greet one another with a holy kiss'. The congregation at Constantinople may well have done so in the way prescribed by the Clementine Liturgy.

There was no singing at this point in the service at this time, so that there was a perhaps considerable pause in the proceedings while the deacons brought in the gifts. It requires a good deal of imagination to realize this in view of the splendour which later came to attend what the Byzantine Liturgy knew as the Great Entrance. But there can be no doubt that the bread and wine were at this time in Constantinople brought in with little ceremony; Chrysostom does not even mention their appearance in his sermons.

The elements had most probably been brought to church by the people. As we have seen, the practice in the East was for them to be deposited somewhere on the way in to church. So far at least as the Great Church in Constantinople is concerned, it is tempting to suppose that they were left in the small round edifice at the north-east corner of Hagia Sofia, which quite probably dates from the time of the first church begun by Constantine.

Known as the skeuophylakion, because the sacred vessels were kept there, it originally had two doors, directly opposite each other, which would have made it easy for the people to pass through, leaving their gifts on the way. It was certainly there that later the preparation of the bread and wine took place before they were brought in at the Great Entrance. However that may be, it is reasonably clear that in Chrysostom's time the gifts were brought in by the deacons from wherever they had been left by the people, and that this transfer was effected in a simple manner. The final stage of their path was probably the solea connecting the ambo with the sanctuary.

The simplicity of this purely practical action, accompanied by neither chant nor ceremonial, is striking not only by comparison with what it later became in the Byzantine Liturgy, but with what it had already become elsewhere. There is a famous description of the entry of the gifts in the *Mystagogical Catecheses* of Theodore of Mopsuestia. Theodore had been a presbyter at Antioch for ten years before becoming Bishop of Mopsuestia, in southern Asia Minor, in 392. Since Chrysostom's sermons preached at Antioch make no mention of the kind of ceremonial described by Theodore, nor of the significance the latter attaches to it, it is probable that the *Catecheses* reflect liturgical practice at Mopsuestia. Because of its importance the passage is worth quoting extensively, though with some abbreviation:

> It is the deacons who bring out this oblation ... which they arrange and place on the awe-inspiring altar, a vision ... awe-inspiring even to the onlookers. By means of the symbols we must see Christ, who is now being led out and going forth to his passion, and who, in another moment, is laid out for us on the altar ... And when the offering that is about to be presented is brought out in the sacred vessels, the patens and chalices, you must think that Christ the Lord is coming out, led to his passion ... by the invisible host of ministers ... who were also present when the passion of salvation was being accomplished ... And when they bring it out, they place it on the holy altar to represent fully the passion. Thus we may think of him placed on the altar as if henceforth in a sort of sepulchre, and as having already undergone the passion. That is why the deacons who spread linens on the altar represent by this the figure of the linen clothes of the burial ... (And afterwards) they stand on both sides and fan the air (*aer*) above the holy Body so that nothing will fall on it. They show by this ritual the greatness of the Body lying there ... which is holy, awe-inspiring and far from all corruption ... a Body that will soon rise to an immortal nature ... It is evident that there were angels beside the tomb, seated on the stone, and now too should one not depict as in an image the similitude of this angelic liturgy? ... (The deacons) stand around and wave their fans ... because the Body lying there is truly Lord by its union with the divine nature. It is with great fear that it must be laid out, viewed and guarded. These things take place in complete silence because, although the Liturgy has not yet begun, still it is fitting to watch the bringing out and depositing of such a great and wonderful object in recollection and fear and a silent and quiet prayer, without saying anything ... and when we see the oblation on the altar as if it were being placed in a kind of sepulchre after death, a great silence falls on those present. Because that which is taking place is awe-inspiring, they must look on it in recollection and fear, since it is suitable that now by the Liturgy ... Christ our Lord rise, announcing to all the

participation in ineffable benefits. We remember therefore the death of the Lord in the oblation because it makes manifest the resurrection and the ineffable benefits. (Cf. Taft, *The Great Entrance*, p. 35.)

Wherever, and for whatever reasons – both are unknown – this interpretation of the entry of the bread and wine was conceived, it was to have a profound influence in the development of the Byzantine Liturgy. It lays great stress on the procession itself, rather than on its objective, and makes it a focus of popular devotion. In making the bread and wine in the procession symbols of Christ going to his death, and on the altar symbols of his dead body, it implies that they are already in some sense sacramental, and so prepares the way for the development of the Byzantine rite of the Prothesis, in which the preparation of the elements in the sacristy before the Liturgy begins represents the passion and death of the Lord. This in turn opens the way to an interpretation of the Eucharist itself as a commemoration of his resurrection. All this was to have far-reaching consequences for the ceremonial development of the Byzantine Liturgy, for the development of its prayers, for the devotional attitude of those taking part in it, and for the iconographic decoration of the churches in which it was celebrated.

But meanwhile, in the Liturgy of early fifth-century Constantinople, the bringing in of the bread and wine retained its original simplicity and practical character. The bishop received them at the altar, and with his clergy prepared to recite the anaphora. First he, and the presbyters with him, washed their hands. Perhaps he also recited a prayer as part of his approach to the altar. We have seen how, in the Clementine Liturgy, the bishop prays by himself, together with the priests, before beginning the eucharistic prayer. Such natural private devotions of the clergy soon became formalized in set prayers incorporated into the Liturgy. The prayers recited in the modern Liturgy appear in the Codex Barberini of the late eighth or early ninth century. There they are called respectively 'The prayer of the proskomidia of St Basil after the people have finished the mystic hymn' and 'The prayer of the proskomidia of St John Chrysostom after the holy gifts have been put on the holy table and after the people have finished the mystic hymn'.

They are prayers of preparation for those about to offer the gifts in the anaphora, which in the fifth century followed immediately, and to which the word 'proskomidia' in the title of the prayers refers. In early Byzantine usage 'proskomidia' denotes the eucharistic prayer, and not the later preliminary preparation of the bread and wine. These are not offertory prayers in the later Western sense, anticipating the anaphora by offering the gifts and asking God to bless them: they are prayers for the officiants, asking God to make them worthy to offer the gifts. The prayer attributed to St John Chrysostom could well be his own composition. That attributed to St Basil seems to be a later, composite prayer. Its first paragraph is a prayer for the officiants, its second has more the character of an offertory prayer.

On which side of the altar did the bishop stand? Traditional Orthodox practice has the celebrant stand at the west side of the altar, facing east, with his back to the people. It is clear that this must have been the case in Constantinople in the fifth century, at least in the two churches where a flight of steps lead from the east side of the altar down into a small crypt where relics were kept. Elsewhere it would certainly have been possible for him to stand at the east side facing the people.

The Eucharistic Prayer

The prayer of preparation finished, the bishop began the anaphora. The introductory dialogue at Constantinople in Chrysostom's time seems to have been the same as in the Clementine Liturgy. The bishop's exhortation after 'The grace of our Lord Jesus Christ . . .' was 'Lift up your minds'. Later it came to be 'Lift up your hearts'. This was the form used in Jerusalem by the latter half of the fourth century, and in the West. In the East the two forms were for some time in competition. In the Liturgy of St James and the Liturgy of the Syrian Jacobites they were combined: 'Lift up your hearts and minds'. In Byzantium by the seventh century 'hearts' had prevailed over 'minds'.

What prayer followed the introductory dialogue? The Codex Barberini contains two Eucharistic liturgies, one ascribed to St Basil, the other without ascription, but containing three prayers ascribed to St John Chrysostom: the prayer for the catechumens, the prayer of the proskomidia, and the final prayer said behind the ambo. It is in fact the Liturgy which came later to be known as that of St John Chrysostom. Of the two Liturgies, that of St Basil is given first, and was at that time the most commonly used.

The anaphora of St Basil is very probably the work of Basil

himself. In his panegyric of Basil, delivered in Caesarea of Cappadocia in 381, Gregory of Nazianzus includes in the great bishop's works the 'reorganization of the Liturgy'. The Belgian scholar Dom Bernard Capelle made a close study of the anaphora of St Basil, comparing it with an Egyptian anaphora also ascribed to him and with Basil's theological writings. He concluded that there was very good reason to suppose that the prayer is in fact his work. Reshaping an existing anaphora, Basil incorporated into his revision his own carefully formulated theological ideas. His anaphora reflects the fully developed trinitarian thought of the latter part of the fourth century, which is henceforth firmly established in the Byzantine liturgical tradition. The Eastern part of the church was far bolder than the Western in allowing its worship to be influenced by current theological thought. In particular the Byzantine Liturgy embodied the view of late fourth-century trinitarian theology that it is the Holy Spirit who sanctifies and consecrates.

If the anaphora of St Basil was the one he himself used in Caesarea, it is not difficult to see how it could have been adopted in Constantinople. The capital was not yet the dominant liturgical centre it was to become, and was open to liturgical influences from outside. The tradition of worship was by no means yet fixed, and the various local traditions interpenetrated one another readily. From 379 to 381 Gregory of Nazianzus, a great friend of Basil's, was Bishop of Constantinople. What more natural than that he should have used there the anaphora used by his friend in Caesarea? The prestige enjoyed by Basil would have made its introduction into the Great Church no difficult matter. His may well then have been the prayer which Chrysostom found in use when he came to Constantinople in 397.

Tradition ascribes to Chrysostom the composition of an anaphora of his own. Liturgical scholarship has by and large discounted this tradition, not least because Chrysostom's name is not firmly linked with the Liturgy now known as his until relatively late. In the Codex Barberini only three prayers are directly ascribed to him. But the question of his authorship of the anaphora has been reopened by Bishop George Wagner. He has compared the content and style of the prayer with Chrysostom's other writings, and concluded that the argument against its authenticity, which is chiefly based on the absence of evidence, is more than balanced by the presence of Chrysostom's own ideas and expressions. Moreover, the title of the prayer 'The prayer of the proskomidia of St John Chrysostom' in the Codex Barberini may well be taken to refer to the anaphora which it immediately preceded as well as to the prayer of preparation itself.

It is of course the case with the Liturgy of St John Chrysostom as with that of St Basil that even if the anaphoras and certain other prayers are held to be by Chrysostom and Basil themselves, other prayers and formulae even in the earliest text of the Liturgies cannot belong to their time. Some are known to have been added later, and others certainly belong to later stages of liturgical development.

Perhaps then worshippers in the Great Church during Chrysostom's episcopate heard the anaphora composed, like Basil's on the basis of existing tradition, by the Archbishop himself. Its use was no doubt discontinued at least for a time after Chrysostom's condemnation, and may have been superseded in the episcopate of Nestorius, whose own anaphora some think was composed in Constantinople. Thereafter for many centuries it took second place to the anaphora of St Basil. The early fifth century was a time when liturgical traditions were still sufficiently fluid for new prayers to be composed and incorporated into a tradition of worship which was not to become rigidly prescribed for several centuries.

In view of subsequent developments it is important to realize that the anaphora was said, or chanted aloud. Not only by reason of its length – especially if Basil's prayer was in use at this time – but by reason of its being virtually the only prayer in the celebration of the sacrament, it dominated the rite, and was its chief verbal explanation. At the beginning of the fifth century the eucharistic liturgy still preserved its original shape and proportions.

The Diptychs

Included in the anaphora were the diptychs of the living and the dead, so called because the lists of names commemorated in the Liturgy were inscribed on two hinged plates, which could be folded together when not in use, and which were kept with the sacred vessels in the skeuophylakion. Considerable significance was already attached to the diptychs in the popular mind, and they were to become still more important in the following centuries. The commemoration of the dead is first attested by Cyril of Jerusalem, and soon spread widely in the East. That of

the living was soon added. In some churches they were read out
before the anaphora began, but there is no reason to think that at
Constantinople they were read elsewhere than in the course of the
intercession within the anaphora. The names in both sets of
diptychs were ranged in hierarchical order, the clergy first, then
the laity. The contents of the diptychs had become by the early
fifth century a matter of great popular interest, and the inclusion
or exclusion of a particular name could arouse fierce passions
among the congregation.

At the beginning of the fifth century the diptychs were chiefly
of interest as showing with which churches or individuals any
given church was in communion. A case in point was that of
Chrysostom himself, after his death in 407. After his deposition
in 404 many of his supporters in Constantinople refused to enter
into communion with his successor Atticus. The latter succeeded
in healing this temporary schism, but then the Johannites complained that John's name was not included in the diptychs of the
dead. Feeling ran high when it was learnt that his name had been
inserted in the diptychs in Antioch, and Atticus, with the
Emperor's consent, bowed to popular pressure and put John's
name into those of the Great Church.

The diptychs were soon to become a test of orthodoxy. In the
doctrinal controversies and consequent schisms, which consumed all too much Christian energy in the next century or two,
individual bishops and churches went in and out of communion
with one another. The diptychs revealed who was considered
orthodox, and who was in communion with whom. At the time of
the Fourth Ecumenical Council at Chalcedon in 451 Bishop
Anatolius of Constantinople was strongly urged by Bishop Leo of
Rome to exclude from the diptychs the names of Dioscorus of
Alexandria, Juvenal of Jerusalem and Eustathius of Berytus, who
had been the leaders in the so-called Robber Synod of Ephesus in
449. One bishop might strike out his predecessor, only to have
him reinstated by his successor. Constantinople might for a time
refuse to commemorate the Bishop of Rome, and vice versa.

It seems that in the East the names on the diptychs were
largely, if not exclusively, those of official persons with ecclesiastical significance. It was bishops and emperors, whether living or
departed, whose names were read out. In the sixth century the
use of diptychs as badges of orthodoxy led to the proposal that the
Ecumenical Councils should be commemorated in them. It seems
that this was first suggested at the Council of Constantinople in

518, with a view to healing a schism between Old Rome and New. The entry of the first four Ecumenical Councils into the diptychs of Constantinople was greeted with wild enthusiasm by the people of the City.

Holy Communion, Thanksgiving and Dismissal

When the people had responded to the eucharistic prayer with their 'Amen', the bishop blessed them with the words: 'Grace and peace be with you'. They replied: 'And with your spirit'. A diaconal litany may well have followed, as in the Clementine Liturgy. The present litany was certainly in the Byzantine rite by the eighth century. The Lord's Prayer, absent from the Clementine rite, had already found its way into that of Constantinople: the first of many communion devotions which were to fill out the simplicity of the early Eucharist at this point.

The bishop invited the people to Communion in the same way as in Jerusalem and the Clementine rite. Raising his hands in a traditional gesture asking for attention he proclaimed: 'Holy things for holy people', and they replied: 'One is holy, one is Lord, Jesus Christ, to the glory of God the Father'. At this time the consecrated gifts themselves were not lifted up. Those in the sanctuary received first, though Chrysostom was at pains to point out that all members of the church are equal when it comes to communicating. The faithful then came forward to receive. The consecrated bread and wine were administered separately, the bread being placed on the right hand, beneath which the left was held. The words of administration were probably 'The Body of Christ', 'The Blood of Christ', to which the communicant replied 'Amen'. We do not know whether the communion devotions recommended by Cyril of Jerusalem had spread to the capital. It is probable that a psalm was sung during Communion.

It is clear from Chrysostom's sermons at Antioch that communion time was far from peaceful, and the same may well have been the case in Constantinople. The doors of the church, closed after the dismissal of the catechumens and penitents, were, it seems, opened immediately Communion began. Not a few took the opportunity of leaving the church, without waiting for the prayer after Communion and the formal dismissal. Since they may well have been in church for some hours, this was not altogether surprising. But there was a more serious reason why some departed. The habit of communicating only once a year was spreading, and those who had no intention of receiving saw no reason why they should stand for some considerable time while the rest partook of the holy gifts.

Consequences of the Decline in Communion

It is one of the more remarkable facts of Christian history that for most of its existence most members of the Church have communicated only rarely, and have sometimes had to be compelled to receive even once a year. In the first three centuries it was out of the question to take part in the celebration of the Eucharist and not to communicate: for Communion was the climax and goal of the service. Regular reception of Communion was the means whereby those incorporated into Christ by baptism were kept in his Body the Church. So important was it that in the second century deacons took Communion from the church gathered for the celebration to the faithful who for good reason were unable to be present themselves.

We have seen the reasons why this attitude to the Eucharist and Communion broke down in the latter part of the fourth century. But the decline in Communion had profound consequences for the liturgy of the Eucharist. In the first three centuries the distribution of Communion formed an important part of the service, and took as long as, if not longer than, the eucharistic prayer. It was also the part of the service in which the people were most fully and actively involved. They had their responses to sing in the psalmody and the litanies. But for most of the service they were listeners, though, it is to be hoped, prayerful ones.

Once the people as a whole ceased to communicate regularly, the balance of the service shifted. Communion occupied a decreasingly prominent part in the rite, and the need to provide the elements also dwindled. The laity became increasingly passive spectators of a service performed by others. The situation was not improved when Cyril of Jerusalem, John Chrysostom and others spoke of the eucharistic sacrifice being accomplished at the end of the anaphora. Communion might follow, but it had come to seem less than integral to the rite.

Without Communion, what was the point of celebrating the Eucharist? Cyril of Jerusalem had emphasized the effectiveness of prayer in the presence of the sacrament, in which was present nothing less than Christ, the victim slain for our salvation. That was why his eucharistic prayer included, after the consecratory epiclesis, a comprehensive intercession for the Church and the world, the living and the dead. Chrysostom took the same view, and this teaching became an integral part of Byzantine and Orthodox doctrine.

But that by itself is not sufficient reason for going to church on Sunday. Further attraction was perhaps provided by the growing splendour of the entry of the bread and wine, and the new significance which Theodore of Mopsuestia and others were coming to attach to it. It may be wondered whether the symbolic interpretation of the Liturgy was not at least in part encouraged by the decline in Communion. It mattered less that people did not receive the Eucharist if they could contemplate in the Liturgy the unfolding story of the life of Christ, or the stages of the soul's ascent to God.

The Understanding of the Eucharist in the Time of Chrysostom

How did the worshippers in the Great Church of the Holy Wisdom understand the Liturgy presided over by John Chrysostom as Archbishop of Constantinople?

Their understanding was first of all shaped by the prayers of the rite, and in particular by the anaphora. If they listened attentively week by week, whether to the anaphora of St Basil, or to that composed by the Archbishop himself, or to any other eucharistic prayer of similar type, they knew that they were engaged in offering a sacrifice of praise and thanksgiving to God for all his mighty acts in creation and redemption, and above all for the passion, death, resurrection and ascension of Jesus Christ, and his coming again in glory. They knew, too, that these saving events were commemorated by the offering of the bread and wine, which through the invocation of the Holy Spirit on them as well as on the worshippers become the Body and Blood of Christ, which they received for the remission of sins and eternal life in God's Kingdom. United with the Mother of God and all the saints they interceded for the living and the departed, and knew themselves to be partakers in the mystical banquet which anticipated the fulfilment of God's plan of salvation.

But the prayers of the Liturgy were not the only formative influence on their understanding of the rite. When they became Christians they attended the bishop's catechetical lectures. These included lectures on the rites of initiation, baptism, chrismation and the Eucharist, such as Cyril of Jerusalem gave. The latter are only the earliest to have survived of a number of similar expositions of the central rites of the Church. Their very existence testifies to the felt need for a fuller explanation of the meaning of baptism and the Eucharist than the prayers used in the course of their celebration provided. Chrysostom himself composed such lectures. In his sermons, too, he conveyed to his hearers an understanding of the Liturgy, which was perhaps more influential than the rite itself in shaping their approach to it.

Chrysostom regularly speaks of the Eucharist as a mystery. In St Paul's writings 'mystery' meant the whole plan of God for our salvation. It has been made known above all in the death and resurrection of Jesus Christ. The concept of mystery later came to be applied to those sacramental actions within the Church which both represented Christ's saving acts, and gave Christians a share in the redemption they had accomplished. Both baptism and the Eucharist were termed mysteries.

Following Origen, Chrysostom calls it a mystery when 'we see one thing and believe another'. What is seen, heard and touched in the Eucharist can be understood by the senses and known by natural reason. But the spiritual, heavenly realities concealed in it can be grasped only by faith and the enlightenment given by the Holy Spirit. The sacrament is a sign of a reality greater than itself, which is nevertheless made present and available in the sign.

Chrysostom frequently speaks of the Eucharist as 'the mysteries' in the plural. Not only does he follow Cyril in qualifying them as fearful and aweful, but he so describes also different parts of the service, the altar, and the hour in which the mysteries are celebrated. Merely to be present is reason for being afraid. Through Chrysostom Cyril's language passed into the Byzantine liturgical and devotional tradition. But Chrysostom was not altogether typical of the period. The Jerusalem Liturgy of St James uses such language freely, and it is found to a lesser extent in the Byzantine Liturgies of Basil and Chrysostom. But the Cappadocian Fathers do not use it, nor is it to be found in the Clementine Liturgy.

In his teaching about the Eucharist Chrysostom makes use of traditional typology, which saw the events of the new covenant prefigured in the old. In the New Testament itself Christ's death and resurrection are seen as the fulfilment of the Exodus. What God did for the Israelites when he led them out of slavery into the promised land pointed forward to that greater Exodus, when through the blood of the true paschal Lamb he brought the whole human race out of slavery to sin into the liberty of his children. The saving acts of Christ are themselves made present in the sacraments, which both enable each generation to appropriate God's salvation, and point forward to its consummation at the end of time. Chrysostom taught his congregation to see the Eucharist prefigured in the sacrifice of Melchisedech, who brought gifts of bread and wine to be offered to God; in the paschal lamb, whose blood daubed on their doorposts saved the Israelites when the first-born of Egypt were slain; in the manna, by which they were sustained in the wilderness; and in the Jewish sacrifices offered under the old covenant.

Chrysostom lays particular stress on the Eucharist as the 'anamnesis' of the many things God has done for us, and especially of the sacrifice of the cross. He urges his congregation to realize that at the Eucharist they are truly in the Upper Room. It is Christ who presides, as at the Last Supper; and when the priest gives them Communion, they must understand it to be the hand of Christ himself which reaches out to them. The Eucharist is an imitation of the death of Christ, and a participation in it. He even uses the Liturgy in this sense to refute heretics who doubt the sacrificial death of Christ: let them be referred to the mysteries, where that sacrifice is present. The incarnation too is present: those who come to the Eucharist in faith will see the Lord lying in the manger, represented by the altar, not wrapped in swaddling clothes but surrounded by the Holy Spirit. He teaches his people to understand the Eucharist as a participation in the worship of heaven. The angels, who are always present in the church, are especially there when the Liturgy is being celebrated.

If Chrysostom makes use of accepted typology, he also employs allegory in explaining the meaning of the Eucharist. The distinction between these two kinds of explanation is important to note in view of later developments in the Byzantine tradition of liturgical interpretation. Typology seeks to explain the meaning of an event in the story of God's dealings with mankind by relating it to another event whose inner meaning is fundamentally similar. So the redemption achieved by Jesus Christ can be seen as fulfilling the Exodus, and the Eucharist can be seen as actualizing the work of Christ, and pointing forward to the final accompaniment of that salvation for the whole of creation towards which God has consistently been working in human history. Typology is concerned with events as entities.

Allegory is concerned rather with the details of events or things, and its interpretation of them can be unrelated to any fundamental similarity of meaning. Its symbolism tends to be arbitrary. There is a hint of this kind of approach when Chrysostom says that the altar represents the manger at Bethlehem. The mystery of Christ present in the Eucharist is beginning to be broken down into its various aspects. Chrysostom says that the incarnation of Christ is made present as well as the passion. When we set that beside Theodore of Mopsuestia's interpretation of the Liturgy, we see the first stage of the tendency to associate different parts of the rite with different moments in the life of Christ.

Symbolic interpretation did not confine itself to the rite itself. Chrysostom relates the altar to the manger. His enthusiastic admirer, Isidore of Pelusium, who may also have been his pupil and who died in 435, explains in one of his letters the meaning of the eileton, or corporal, the deacon's stole and the bishop's omophorion. The interpretation given in the following passages passed into the Byzantine tradition of liturgical explanation:

> The unfolding of the pure eileton under the holy oblations signifies the ministry of Joseph of Arimathea. He wrapped the body of the Lord in a linen cloth and laid it in a tomb whence came resurrection for all our race. In the same way we consecrate the bread which has been offered on the eileton and we find there with certainty the Body of the Lord, the source of that immortality which Jesus, laid in the tomb by Joseph, has bestowed on us by his resurrection (*Letter* 1.123).

> The orarion with which the deacons accomplish their ministry in the sanctuary recalls the humility of the Lord, who washed the feet of his disciples and wiped them. The omophorion of the bishop is made of wool and not of linen: for it signifies the fleece of the lost sheep for which the Lord sought and which he placed on his shoulders. The bishop, in fact, is a figure of Christ. He fulfils his functions, and shows us by his vestment that he is imitating the good and great shepherd, who offered to bear himself the infirmities of his flock (*Letter* 1.136).

The source of allegorical interpretation of the Liturgy seems to have been in the region of Antioch. The first such systematic explanation is that of Theodore of Mopsuestia in his *Catechetical Homilies*. While he uses typology in his exegesis of Scripture, he does not attempt to relate the Eucharist to any Old Testament prefiguration. For him the Liturgy is the image of heavenly realities, and the memorial of the historical life of Jesus.

Explaining the Eucharist as the memorial of the life of Jesus, Theodore concentrates on his death and resurrection. He relates the different aspects of those events to successive stages in the rite. The procession accompanying the entry of the bread and wine represents Christ's going forth to his sacrificial death. The deacons are the angels who supported him during his passion. The placing of the bread and wine on the altar recall the deposition of Christ's body in the tomb. The silence of the people during the anaphora represents the silence of the stunned disciples, or that of the angels, waiting for the resurrection. The coming of the Holy Spirit in response to the epiclesis symbolizes the return of Christ's spirit to his body. The breaking of the bread recalls the resurrection appearances of Jesus.

This breakdown of the eucharistic memorial, or anamnesis, of Jesus' saving passion into a detailed commemoration of its successive stages reflects a similar breakdown of its yearly celebration in the Paschal feast. Until the fourth century the death and resurrection of Jesus were celebrated together on one day at Easter. The celebration was less a commemoration of a past event than a participation in the present reality of redemption. Through the sacraments of baptism and the Eucharist, celebrated in the course of the Easter Vigil, the death of Jesus and his resurrection to eternal life were reproduced in the sacramental death in the font of the members of his Body, the Church, and their participation in his risen life. Holy Week as a detailed commemoration of the events of the last week of Jesus' life came into being towards the end of the fourth century in Jerusalem. Perhaps it was Cyril of Jerusalem himself who devised the pattern of processions and services which enabled pilgrims as well as local Christians to commemorate these events in the places and at the times at which they had happened. The single comprehensive celebration of the first three centuries became a series of dramatic services commemorating the successive stages of Christ's suffering, death, burial and resurrection. They are described in detail by Egeria, who visited the Holy Land as a pilgrim from the west in the early 380s. The background to their emergence was the new interest in the details of the earthly life of

Jesus, associated with the Empress Helena's visit to the Holy Land in 326 and her son Constantine's lavish building programme, which covered the principal holy sites with magnificent churches.

By the end of the fourth century the eucharistic memorial of Jesus, like the Paschal celebration, was beginning to be understood less in a sacramental, and more in a dramatic, historical way. This tendency was strengthened as this particular tradition of interpretation developed. It had a profound influence on every aspect of Byzantine eucharistic worship: it was given expression in prayers added to the rite; it inspired a wealth of ceremonial development; it helped to shape the late Byzantine iconographic scheme of church decoration; and it had a lasting effect on Orthodox eucharistic piety.

5 The Liturgy in the time of Maximus the Confessor

In the two centuries that followed Chrysostom's occupation of the see of Constantinople a number of developments took place in the celebration of the Liturgy in the capital. The Great Church itself, damaged in the disturbances which accompanied Chrysostom's expulsion from his bishopric in 404, was finally destroyed in the Nike riots under Justinian in 532, and replaced by the magnificent new Hagia Sofia, the mother church of Byzantine Christianity and increasingly the model for Byzantine liturgical worship. The new Great Church provided the architectural setting for a rite which during these centuries was steadily receiving additions to its prayers and other formulae, and whose ceremonial was steadily evolving. We have information from various sources about these developments, which produced the rite upon which Maximus the Confessor commented in his *Mystagogia* early in the seventh century, and to which he is the chief witness.

These developments took place against a background of continuing doctrinal controversy, which was not without its effect on the Liturgy in Constantinople, where the population took a lively interest in both doctrine and worship. Debate focused on the doctrine of the person of Jesus Christ, to which the theological traditions of Alexandria and Antioch took differing approaches. The former tended to emphasize the divinity of Christ, at what some thought to be the cost of his full humanity. The latter so emphasized the completeness of his humanity, that for others there was a less than perfect union of the two natures in the person of Jesus Christ. Early in the fifth century Nestorius, Patriarch of Constantinople, doubted the appropriateness of calling Mary Theotokos, or Mother of God. As an Antiochene he preferred Christotokos. The Third Ecumenical Council of Ephesus in 431 affirmed the correctness of applying Theotokos to Mary, and the title passed into frequent liturgical use in the Byzantine tradition, always quick to reflect contemporary dogmatic definition.

67

The definition of the Fourth Ecumenical Council of Chalcedon in 451, proclaiming the union of the divine and human natures in the one person of Jesus Christ, was an attempt to reconcile the Alexandrian and Antiochene traditions in Christology. For political as well as doctrinal reasons the definition was unacceptable to those who eventually came to be called monophysite on the one side, and Nestorian on the other. Meanwhile in the latter part of the fifth century monophysite tendencies were influential throughout the Eastern part of the Church, and found imperial support. The accession of the Emperor Justin in 518 put a stop to this trend. The four ecumenical councils were included in the diptychs read at the Liturgy, and the names of the recent pro-monophysite patriarchs of the capital removed.

Under Justinian a policy designed to reconcile the monophysites to Chalcedonian orthodoxy was pursued. Leontius of Byzantium elaborated the view that while the humanity of Christ had no hypostasis, or centre of personal being, of its own, it found its centre in the hypostasis of the divine Word: it was enhypostatic. The Fifth Ecumenical Council of Constantinople in 553 gave its authority to Leontius' teaching. At the same time it condemned aspects of the teaching of Theodore of Mopsuestia, Theodoret, and Ibas of Edessa, whose followers had protested against Leontius' doctrine, and so finally divided the East Syrian Christians of Persian Mesopotamia from the Byzantine Church. Their Church of the East was called Nestorian by the orthodox.

At the same time monophysites began to form separate Churches, both within the Empire and outside its frontiers: the independent existence of the Coptic and Syrian Churches dates from this period. The imperial authorities attempted to find a basis for reconciliation by suggesting that, though there may be two natures, there is only one energy in Jesus Christ, both human and divine. But monoenergism was unacceptable to the strict Chalcedonians, as too was the monothelete doctrine that developed out of the controversy surrounding it. Maximus the Confessor was, with Patriarch Sophronius of Jerusalem, one of their leaders in resisting imperial attempts to force the doctrine of one will in Christ on the Church of the Empire. It was for refusing to obey the imperial edict of 648 forbidding all discussion of the matter while leaving the doctrinal issue unresolved that Maximus suffered first exile and then the amputation of his tongue and right hand. Meanwhile he spent some time in Rome, where he helped to formulate the doctrine of two operations and two wills

in Christ, which eventually received the approval of the Sixth
Ecumenical Council of Constantinople in 680–1.

Justinian's Church of the Holy Wisdom

In the course of the fifth century a number of churches were built
in Constantinople. Sufficient has been discovered by archaeol-
ogists about three of them to provide some idea of their interior
layout. Their general plan was similar to that of the original
fourth-century Hagia Sofia.

The sixth century saw the extensive building programme of the
Emperor Justinian, which included in the City a large number of
churches in addition to the masterpiece of the new Hagia Sofia.
Enough of them have survived to enable us to form a reasonably
good idea of the setting in which the Liturgy was celebrated in
Justinian's time, and for several centuries after. Some were built

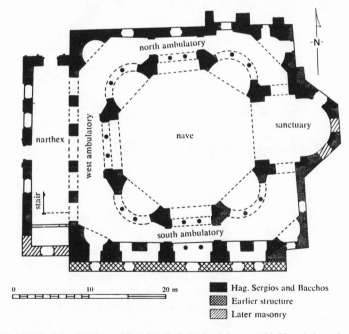

*The church of Ss. Sergios and Bacchos, built by Justinian near his Hormisdas palace,
and probably finished by 536.*

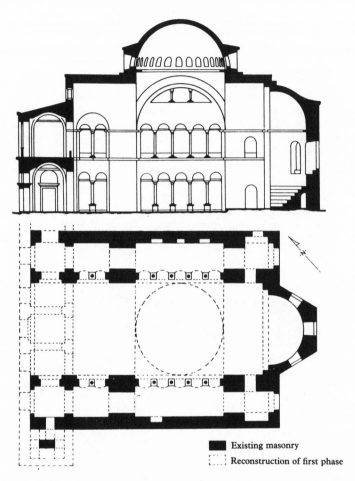

Longitudinal section and plan of Hagia Eirene, as first built by Justinian at the same time as Hagia Sophia.

in the basilican style. Others were of a new centrally-planned type, whose domed central space was surrounded by ambulatories and galleries. Some, like Hagia Sofia itself, combined a central dome with a rectangular ground plan. St Sergius and St Bacchus, still standing, though used as a mosque, has an octagonal nave, surrounded on most sides by an ambulatory below and galleries above. To the east the sanctuary extends from the nave into a

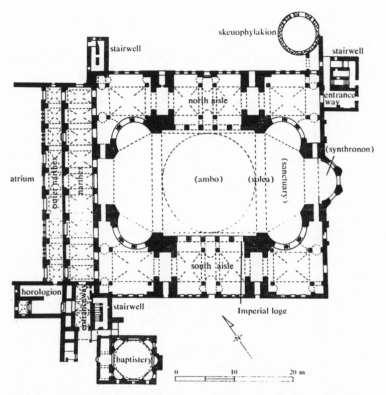

Plan of the Great Church of Hagia Sophia, Holy Wisdom, dedicated by Justinian in 537.

semicircular apse. It closely resembles the church of San Vitale in Ravenna. Similar to both was the church of St John the Forerunner in the Hebdomon suburb of Constantinople. Hagia Eirene, on the other hand, most of which has survived, had a rectangular ground plan, with a sanctuary apse at the east end. The six stone benches of its synthronon are still in place in the apse. As in Hagia Sofia the central portion of the nave is covered by an immense dome. Like most of the Constantinopolitan churches, it had a narthex at the west end, which was entered from an atrium.

It was the new Hagia Sofia that dominated not only the city but the whole Eastern Empire. It stands now substantially as it was built by Justinian's architects, Anthemius and Isidore. To the west of the church was an atrium, which survived into the seventeenth century but had largely disappeared two centuries later. It was entered through large doors in the north and south sides, and had an arcade running round three sides. The fourth side was the outer narthex of the church. In the middle of the open courtyard stood a large marble fountain. It seems that the church had open courtyards on its other sides too, which enabled the light to penetrate unhindered into the building, and also provide space for the people to gather.

From the atrium five doors led into the outer narthex, three in the centre, one at either end. The remaining four bays were filled with windows. A similar pattern of doors leads into the inner narthex, from which nine doors give access to the church itself. From the inner narthex two doors, to north and south, lead into vestibules, one at each end, from which a large door opens onto the ramp which leads to the galleries above. The northern vestibule is a later Turkish addition. The southern vestibule too was probably an addition, though made before the eighth century. Originally the inner narthex, and the ramps as well, were approached directly from outside. It seems that to begin with there were also ramps at the north-east and south-east corners of the church, so that the galleries had four means of access, all approached from outside the building. A fifth stair was subsequently built outside the south-west pier, giving access to a section of the south gallery that was separated from the rest by a barrier.

Further entrances into the church were provided in the north and south walls, and also on the east side, on either side of the sanctuary apse. It is important to realize that there was only one apse at the east end of Hagia Sofia: there was no smaller flanking apse of the kind that later became standard in Byzantine church design, and served as diaconicon and prothesis. The central nave, rectangular in shape and covered by the huge central dome and the two supporting semi-domes, is flanked to north and south by aisles and galleries, each divided into three large bays by arches. The aisles open directly into the nave along the whole of their length. A section of the south aisle was originally screened by barriers to protect the Emperor's box.

Although the new Great Church incorporated new architectural features, its layout was basically conservative, and resembled that of earlier churches in the city. Not a great deal of evidence remains for reconstructing the arrangements of the sanctuary, which was restored three times before its final destruction by the Turks. From the description given by Paul the Silentiary after its restoration following the collapse of the dome in 558 some impression of it can be built up. Round the apse the synthronon rose in seven steps: only the topmost bench was intended as seating, and its seats were of silver. The altar had a base, columns and top all of gold, ornamented with precious stones. It was surmounted by a silver ciborium. Its precise place is unknown: it may have been forward of the chord of the apse, for the sanctuary platform almost certainly projected beyond the apse into the nave. It was protected by chancel slabs, set into twelve columns which rose above them to support an architrave, on which were set images of Christ, the Virgin, apostles and angels. There were three entrances to the sanctuary, one in the centre, and one on each side.

From a little in front of the central entrance a solea, with low barriers, led to the great ambo, set in the middle of the nave, a little to the east of centre. Its oval platform rested on eight columns, and was large enough for the cantors to be stationed beneath it. Steps led up to it from east and west. The whole structure was enclosed by eight columns bearing an architrave, with chancel barriers between them.

The liturgical arrangements of Justinian's Great Church were those which had been characteristic of the city's churches for the past two centuries. But if it was conservative in this respect, the new Hagia Sofia marked the beginning of a new era in Byzantine church design. In particular the dome became a characteristic of Byzantine churches, and came to play a central part in the interpretation of the building itself as a symbol of spiritual realities. The interpretation of the dome as heaven was known before its use in Hagia Sofia. Although there is no need to see its use there as a deliberate attempt to incorporate its symbolism into the new building, it lent itself readily to the growing tendency to ascribe symbolic significance to the structure of the church.

Procopius' description of the new Great Church shows the impression it produced on those who first entered it. The interior

is too splendid to appear ordinary and too tastefully decorated to appear excessively rich. It is bathed in sunlight and the reflection of the sun's rays; one might almost say that it is not illuminated from without by the sun but that the radiance originates from within, so inundated with light is this

sanctuary ... Upon this circle (the arcades with the pendentives) rises a sort of huge, spherical dome, an incomparably
beautiful structure; it seems not so much to rest upon the solid
substructure, as to cover the space with its golden dome
suspended from heaven. And all this is fitted together on high
with extraordinary harmony – one thing depends on the other
and finds support only in what lies directly beneath, so that the
total effect is exceedingly impressive, yet the eye of the specta-
tor does not linger long on any one detail. Each detail attracts
the gaze and draws it irresistibly to itself. Thus the eye
constantly springs suddenly from one thing to another and the
beholder finds it impossible to decide what pleases him most.
Even they who are accustomed to exercise their ingenuity on
everything are unable to comprehend this work of art but
always depart from there perplexed at the shortcomings of eye
and mind ... If anyone enters to pray, then ... his mind is
lifted up and he walks in heaven; he thinks that God cannot be
far away and that he gladly dwells in this place which he
himself has chosen (Procopius, *On Buildings*, I, 1, 29–30, 45–9,
61–3).

All Justinian's churches were no doubt richly decorated,
although practically no original mosaics have been left in Constantinople, except perhaps for some aisle vaulting decoration in
Hagia Sofia. The basilican churches of the fifth century began to
be decorated in accordance with a consistent scheme. The walls
of the nave had on one side a sequence of New Testament scenes,
matched on the other side with corresponding scenes from the
Old Testament. The separate panels had rich mosaic frames. Any
space between or around them was filled in with decorative
patterns. Vaults were normally filled with conventional designs.
Most striking of all were the figures in the semi-dome of the apse,
which was not yet the almost exclusive preserve of the Mother of
God. Christ Pantocrator, perhaps with apostles, was sometimes
there, or the saint in whose honour the church was dedicated. In
the sixth-century Basilica of the monastery of St Catherine in
Sinai the transfiguration is depicted. While most of the upper
part of the church was covered with mosaic, the lower part of the
walls and pillars was generally covered with rich marble slabs,
whose veining contributed enormously to their decorative value.
A sixth-century example of the decoration of a basilican
church is provided by the church of San Apollinare Nuovo at

Ravenna, the seat of Byzantine government in Italy at that time. On the north side of the nave a procession of men saints, led by the three Magi, moves from west to east to offer homage to the Christ-child enthroned with Mary. On the south side a parallel procession of holy women comes to pay homage to the enthroned Christ. Between the windows above them are figures of the prophets, while above the windows small panels illustrate, on the north the teaching of Christ, and on the south his passion. Both sequences are linked with the biblical lectionary used then in the church.

The mosaics that have survived in San Vitale in Ravenna give a good impression of sixth-century decoration of the sanctuary of such a centrally-planned church. The upper part of the walls and the vaulting are covered with mosaic. In the semi-dome of the apse is a representation of Christ and his cortège. On the north wall is the famous representation of Justinian entering the church with Archbishop Maximian, on the south the Empress Theodora, both escorted by clergy and members of the court. In the vault four standing angels support a central medallion with the Lamb in it, while on the arch leading into the sanctuary two flying angels carry a medallion inscribed with a cross. The remaining space on the walls is filled with scenes from the life of Moses on the north, Old Testament figures of the Eucharist – Melchisedech bringing out bread and wine, and the sacrifice of Isaac – on the south, and by figures of prophets, evangelists, angels and saints. Floral and animal motifs mingle with other decorative patterns to fill the gaps between the main scenes.

One tendency in sixth-century representational decoration must be noticed. The practice of representing sacred figures facing the beholder originated in the religious art of Eastern Hellenism, in northern Mesopotamia or in Iran. It spread through Parthian influence into Syria and Anatolia, and exercised a decisive influence on Byzantine religious art. In sixth-century decoration its influence can be seen alongside the continuing Greek tradition of decorative art. But from the latter part of the sixth century onwards its influence came more and more to predominate. Its intention was to depict the figure as present to the beholder, who through the image could enter into a relationship with the person represented. It was from this tradition that the Byzantine theology of the icon was formed in the heat of the eighth-century iconoclastic controversy. Its influence can be seen in the sixth-century mosaics in the apse of San Apollinare in

Classe in Ravenna, and in the next century in the representations of St Demetrios in Thessalonike.

As this tendency grew stronger, it gradually drove out the rich variety of Greek decorative designs and patterns. The fully-frontal figure stood out against a severely plain background, and the older narrative compositions began to disappear from church decoration, though it was not until after the iconoclastic controversy that a new, coherent pattern of decoration emerged.

The Liturgy of the Eucharist and its Ceremonial

At the beginning of the fifth century the Eucharist was celebrated by and large in Constantinople with its early simplicity. The structure of the rite was clearly visible, and still retained its balance of word and sacrament. That was still the case at the beginning of the seventh century. But in the intervening two centuries a number of additions were made to the order of service, in Constantinople as in other churches, both Eastern and Western.

The Entry into the Church

In Maximus' time the Liturgy still began with the entry of the celebrant and the people into the church. As the Great Church, or at one of the other major churches of the city, the Emperor, on such occasions as he took a formal part in the Liturgy, arrived with his court in the narthex, and sat waiting for the patriarch. They entered the church together, at the head of the congregation. It is probable that the mosaic panels in San Vitale in Ravenna depict precisely this entry of Emperor and patriarch into the church: the Emperor and Empress carry with them the gifts custom prescribed they should offer on such occasions. The people then poured into the church through all available doors. It is not surprising to find that Hagia Sofia had one hundred doorkeepers on its staff.

The text of the Liturgy of St John of Chrysostom in the later Codex Barberini contains a Prayer of Entry, which in the late eighth century was said at what came to be called the Little Entrance, when after the introductory antiphons and litanies the clergy entered the sanctuary. It differs from the modern prayer, which is that of the Liturgy of St Basil in the Codex Barberini. It runs:

Benefactor and Creator of all creation, receive the Church which is advancing, accomplish what is good for each one: bring all to perfection, make us worthy of your Kingdom; by the grace and mercy and love for men of your only-begotten Son, with whom you are blessed, together with your holy and good and life-giving Spirit, now and always, etc.

This prayer fits exactly the situation in which the entry of the whole congregation into the church is the beginning of the service, and was in all probability said out loud by the bishop in the narthex immediately before he led the people in.

The Entry Chant

The entry in New Rome stood in contrast with that in Old Rome, where the people assembled in church to greet the bishop as he arrived. But in New Rome as in old, the entry was no longer made in silence. In the fifth century chant was introduced to accompany the entry of the clergy, and in Constantinople of the people after them. It consisted of a psalm, accompanied by a refrain, or troparion. The troparion was first repeated three times by the chanters, and then the people sang it three times. The whole troparion, or its final part, was then sung after every few verses of the psalm and after the 'Glory be to the Father' at the end. The whole refrain was repeated once more by the chanters, and finally by the people.

Early in the sixth century the refrain to the entry chant in Constantinople was the Trisagion: 'Holy (is) God, holy and strong, holy and immortal! Have mercy on us'. The monk Job who provides this information may well have been right when he explained the text as made up of the 'Holy, holy, holy' of the cherubim in Isaiah 6.2 and of verse 3 of Psalm 41 in the liturgical psalter then in use which describes God as 'strong' and 'living', the latter having been replaced by 'immortal'. The present manner of singing the Trisagion, from which the psalm itself has long since disappeared, represents the initial threefold repetition of the refrain, the 'Glory be' at the end of the psalm, the repetition of the final clause of the refrain, and a single repetition of the whole. Traces of the psalm remain in the Trisagion sung at an episcopal Liturgy: the bishop uses parts of verses 15 and 16 of Psalm 79 (80) in between the repetitions while blessing the congregation. The alternation of choir and clergy in chanting the

Trisagion when the bishop celebrates corresponds to the ancient alternation of chanters and people.

The chant, 'As many as have been baptized into Christ have put on Christ. Alleluia!', sung instead of the Trisagion on certain festivals, has a similar origin. At one time it was sung on Holy Saturday as the refrain between the verses of Psalm 31 (32) during the procession which conducted the newly-baptized from the baptistry to the church for the Eucharist. Both chants still mark the beginning of the Liturgy on certain days, such as Holy Thursday and Holy Saturday, when it is immediately preceded by another service.

There is evidence to suggest that at the end of the fifth century the Trisagion was considered suitable for use as the refrain to psalms sung in rogation processions – acts of solemn intercession in times of trouble. The verses of Psalm 79 (80) sung by the bishop when he blesses the people during the Trisagion may derive from this custom. They were originally sung by the deacon, and perhaps represent the end of the processional psalm, sung as the procession entered the church.

This use of the Trisagion may be reflected in the legendary story of its first introduction into liturgical use. In the time of Patriarch Proclus (434–46) the people of Constantinople were engaged in fervent prayer during a severe earthquake. A young boy was rapt up to the third heaven, where he heard the angels singing the Trisagion. The people were told to sing it, and when they did so the earthquake ceased. The story may at any rate point to the time when it first began to be used liturgically in the capital. It was certainly well known by 451, when the Eastern bishops sang it as an acclamation at the Fourth Ecumenical Council.

Perhaps then to begin with the Trisagion was used only when the Liturgy was preceded by a procession of a penitential, intercessory character. On other occasions variable troparia may have served as refrains to the psalm sung during the procession to the church where the Liturgy was to be celebrated, or simply at the entry into the church. In time the Trisagion, ultimately detached from any psalm, became a fixed chant in the Liturgy, preceded by the entrance psalm used on other occasions which eventually became the third antiphon of the enarxis, and followed by the variable troparia, equally detached from the psalm they had originally accompanied.

The Trisagion soon became a focal point of doctrinal controversy. In the early years of his episcopate at Antioch the mono-physite Patriarch Peter the Fuller (468/70–88) added to it the phrase, 'who was crucified for us'. He clearly understood the Trisagion to be addressed to the second Person of the Trinity, the incarnate Word. The addition reflected the monophysite insist-ence, following the Alexandrian tendency in Christology, that it was perfectly proper to say that God died for us, because the 'I' in Jesus Christ was the divine Word. The followers of Theodore of Mopsuestia, on the other hand, were still hesitant about the appropriateness of calling Mary 'Theotokos', and so of saying that God was born. The addition was adopted in monophysite circles, but was fiercely contested by the orthodox Chalcedonian Byzantines. Byzantine interpretation of the Trisagion referred it to the Trinity: 'Holy God' to the Father, 'holy and strong' to the Son, 'holy and immortal' to the Spirit. The controversy between orthodox and monophysite points of view continued for some centuries. It flared up in the capital when in 513 the Emperor Anastasius ordered the addition to be sung in the church of St Theodore of Sphorakios close to the Great Church.

It may be that historically neither was correct, and that to begin with the Trisagion was meant to be addressed to God, principally as Father, exactly like the liturgical Sanctus in the eucharistic prayer. This seems to have been the way in which it was understood by the composer of the Prayer of the Trisagion found in the Liturgy of St Basil in the Codex Barberini. This prayer is now common to both Liturgies, although in the Codex Barberini a different prayer is provided for the Liturgy of St John Chry-sostom. Both prayers are addressed primarily to the God who loves mankind and has mercy on him, that is, to the Father. Of course the Christian belief that God is Trinity is always present. But neither of these prayers suggests that their authors thought of the Trisagion they accompanied as addressed specifically to the Trinity. The trinitarian doxology at the end of each prayer may well be a late addition, reflecting the Byzantine tendency to make all doxologies trinitarian.

At this time, and perhaps for some time before, the entry procession was led by a deacon carrying the book of the Gospels, escorted by candles and incense. The Gospels, symbol of Jesus Christ, the Word of God, were enthroned on the altar when the procession reached the sanctuary. As earlier, the bishop and his clergy mounted the synthronon in the apse, and when the bishop had given the greeting 'Peace be with you all' took their seats for the scripture readings. The procession in the Great Church must have taken some time – hence the need for an entry chant of some length.

The Readings and Sermon

In the seventh century the readings followed immediately after the entry. There were still three of them, from the Old Testament, from the Epistles, and from the Gospels. Between the readings psalms were chanted, with antiphons before and after, and between the verses. For these the cantors ascended the ambo. The first two readings were read by lectors, of whom the Great Church had one hundred and ten in Justinian's time, and one hundred and sixty in that of Heraclius, in the first half of the seventh century. The reading of the Gospel was certainly by this time accompanied by the splendour due to this manifestation of the presence of Christ in and to his Church. The Gospel book itself was richly covered with precious metals and stones. Candles and incense escorted it as the deacon carried it to the ambo, and on his return to the sanctuary along the solea the people pressed forward to venerate it. In his description of Hagia Sofia, restored after the collapse of the first dome in 538, Paul the Silentiary writes of the solea and its protecting barriers:

> Now for these fence walls they have not placed lofty slabs, but they are as high as the navel of a man passing by them; and here the gospeller, as he holds the golden Gospel, passes along, and the surging crowd strives to touch the sacred book with their lips and hands, while moving waves of people break around.

Liturgical celebration in Constantinople was never dull.

It may be that by the seventh-century preaching had declined in Constantinople. Maximus the Confessor does not mention a homily in his exposition of the rite. The Council 'in Trullo' of 692 lays it down that bishops should preach every day, but especially on Sunday. Since what is already being done does not have to be enforced, we may presume that at least some bishops were neglecting their duty, even on Sundays. Justinian's repetition of a law of the Emperor Theodosius, which proclaimed it sacrilegious for a bishop to preach inaccurately or not at all suggests that Chrysostom's high standards in this respect did not long survive him. There is certainly no body of sermons comparable to his from the sixth or seventh centuries in Constantinople.

That is not to say sermons were never preached. But it was clearly possible to go to church and not hear one.

The Dismissals and Prayers of the Faithful

After the readings, or the homily if there was one, the customary prayers for the catechumens were said before they were dismissed, and the doors of the church closed. The discipline of penance had fallen into disuse by the seventh century, and since there were no penitents to dismiss the prayers said on their behalf had dropped out. It may be wondered how vigorous the catechumenate was in Constantinople at this time, or whether the prayers for the catechumens were not already an anachronism. Since the Liturgy was still at this time capable of receiving additions, we may suppose that it was also still capable of rejecting elements that no longer expressed the actual life of the Church. The catechumenate may have survived, even if in an attenuated form, to provide for converts from the many foreigners who had business in the city. By the time the catechumenate finally disappeared, the Church had become too rigid in its attitudes to allow the redundant prayers to disappear too.

Although there is no mention of the prayers of the faithful in Maximus' *Mystagogia*, it may be presumed that, in the form of a diaconal litany, they still had their place in the rite after the dismissal of the catechumens.

The Entrance of the Mysteries

There is no doubt that in the seventh century the bread and wine for the Eucharist were, at the Great Church, brought in from the skeuophylakion which stood near the northeast corner of the church. Similar architectural arrangements existed at other churches in the City. In the skeuophylakion the holy vessels and books were kept, and here too the clergy prepared themselves and the gifts of the people for the service. Small churches as well as large had their separate skeuophylakia.

The deacons went to the skeuophylakion while the bishop was reciting the prayer for the catechumens. Having collected the paten and chalice, or patens and chalices, they returned, escorted by candles, incense and fans. Their precise route is not certain. They may, at the Great Church, have passed along the outside of the building along the north wall, and entered the church by the great door in the middle of the north side; or they may have entered the church at the east end of the north aisle and passed along it to its mid-point, turning into the nave in order to reach the solea by the ambo. Certainly they passed down the solea to the sanctuary. The bishop meanwhile waited to receive the gifts at the altar. When the Emperor attended the Liturgy officially he came to meet the procession at the entrance to the solea, and accompanied the procession as far as the holy door in the middle of the chancel barrier. He then returned to his place in the south aisle.

The procession with the gifts was clearly a prominent feature of the rite, and at any rate by the sixth century the ideas we have already seen expressed in Theodore of Mopsuestia's *Catechetical Lectures* had become popular in Constantinople too. They were not without their critics. In his sermon on the Paschal feast and the holy Eucharist Eutychius, Patriarch of Constantinople 552–5, 577–82, disapproves strongly of the popular reverence displayed to the bread and wine as they pass through the church:

> They act stupidly, who have taught the people to sing a certain psalmic chant when the ministers are about to bring up to the altar the bread of oblation and the recently-mixed chalice. In this hymn, which they consider suitable to the action being performed, the people say that they bear in the King of glory, and refer in this way to things being brought up, even though they have not yet been consecrated by the high-priestly invocation – unless perhaps what is sung means something else to them. For as Athanasius the Great says in his sermon to the baptized: 'You will see the Levites (i.e. the deacons) bearing in bread and a chalice of wine and putting them on the table. And as long as the supplications and the prayer have not been completed, it is nothing but plain bread' (Taft, *The Great Entrance*, p. 84).

Eutychius' strictures on misplaced popular devotion reveal that the entrance of the gifts was accompanied by singing. In all the churches the fifth century saw the introduction of chant here, as well as at the beginning of the Liturgy. It was usually a psalm with a popular refrain. Eutychius' remarks seem to point to this as the form taken by the chant in Constantinople, since he speaks of it as a psalmic chant. Moreover his reference to the King of glory suggests the use of Psalm 24, in which psalm alone the phrase occurs. On the basis of all available evidence it seems likely that in the early sixth century the chant that accompanied the entrance of the gifts was Psalm 24, verses 7–10, probably with 'Alleluia' as the refrain.

Later in the sixth century the present Cherubic Hymn was added. The historian Cedrenus says that the Emperor Justin II decreed that it should be sung, in the ninth year of his reign (573–4), presumably at the entry of the mysteries. At the same time it was decreed that on Holy Thursday the hymn, 'At your mystical supper,' should be sung. The only other hymn now used at the Great Entrance is that sung on Holy Saturday, 'Let all mortal flesh be silent'. This hymn seems to have been introduced into the rite of Constantinople only much later, in the eleventh or twelfth century. It may have been borrowed from the Liturgy of Jerusalem, and was at first an optional alternative on Holy Saturday to the Cherubic Hymn.

When the Cherubicon and other troparia were introduced, it was almost certainly as refrains to the psalm, attached to the earlier refrain 'Alleluia'. The whole chant would have been sung in the same way as the entry chant. The troparion was sung three times by the chanters, and then three times by the people. The chanters then sang the psalm verses, and in between them the people sang the final phrase of the troparion, in the case of the Cherubicon 'Alleluia', in that of the Holy Thursday troparion 'Remember me, Lord, in your Kingdom'. After the 'Glory be' the final phrase was sung, followed by the whole troparion sung by the chanters, and repeated by the people. Such a lengthy chant was of course necessary to accompany the procession in the Great Church. Fewer verses of the psalm might suffice in smaller churches, where too the priests and deacons might have to take over the role of the chanters. Few if any churches had the services of so large a range of singers as Hagia Sofia.

While the deacons were bringing in the mysteries with a good deal of solemnity, the bishop was preparing to receive them. At this time it was probably during the procession that he, and perhaps the presbyters with him, washed his hands in a symbolic gesture of purity, and said in a low voice the prayer in preparation for the anaphora. When the deacons arrived, the gifts were set in order on the altar, and may have been censed.

It is important to realize that the chant at the entry of the mysteries in the Byzantine rite forms an introduction to the whole of the subsequent part of the Liturgy, and is not just an accompaniment to the procession with the gifts. It has commonly come to be understood in the light of the fully-developed symbolic interpretation of the Liturgy as referring to the coming of Christ, represented by the gifts, in the procession itself. But the texts themselves show that they have a wider bearing. The Cherubic Hymn urges the worshippers to lay aside every worldly care so as to be ready to receive Christ in Communion. It looks forward to the singing of the Sanctus, the thrice-holy hymn of the angels. The chant for Holy Thursday is in fact a communion chant, emphasizing still more the relation between the chant at the Great Entrance and all that is to follow. The Holy Saturday chant speaks of Christ coming forth to be slain and given as food to the faithful, again looking forward to Communion.

The Cherubic Hymn and the Holy Saturday chant reflect the common Eastern view, popularized by Dionysius the Areopagite, that the earthly liturgy is a reflection of the heavenly: Christ, symbolized by the bread and wine, is escorted by angels, represented by the deacons. In these chants the symbolism first found in Theodore of Mopsuestia found its way into the Liturgy in Constantinople. The Holy Saturday chant in particular is very close to Theodore in its content.

The gifts now placed on the altar, the bishop gave his greeting: 'Peace be with you all', and the kiss of peace was exchanged, as earlier, by both clergy and people. But by the seventh century the anaphora no longer followed immediately.

The Creed

By the time of Maximus the creed now commonly called Nicene, the symbol of 'the one hundred and fifty fathers assembled in Constantinople' in 381 for the Second Ecumenical Council, was already well-established in the Liturgy. Its text made its first appearance in the Acts of the Fourth Ecumenical Council held at Chalcedon in 451. Its function there was to serve as an expression of orthodox belief both as regards the doctrine of God as Trinity and as regards that of the person of Christ. It is probably an adapted version of a local baptismal creed, for the original context in which credal forms developed was that of initiation into membership of the Church.

Creeds certainly played no part in the early liturgy of the Eucharist. Exactly when, where and why the creed was introduced into the service is unclear. Peter the Fuller, the monophysite Patriarch of Antioch towards the end of the fifth century, is said to have started the practice there in 473. A passage of Theodore the Lector's *Ecclesiastical History* relates that

> Timothy (Patriarch of Constantinople 511–18) ordered that the symbol of faith of the three hundred and eighteen fathers be recited at each synaxis out of disparagement for Macedonius, as if he did not accept the symbol. Formerly it was recited only once a year, on Good Friday, at the bishop's catechesis (cf. Taft, ibid, p. 398).

The three hundred and eighteen fathers were the members of the First Ecumenical Council of 325. This need not be taken to mean that the creed introduced by Timothy was not the formula agreed in 381, but the earlier one of 325. The creed used in Constantinople in the rite of baptism since 451 had been what is now called the Nicene Creed (but should more accurately be called the Nicene-Constantinopolitan Creed) and there is no evidence that any other was ever used at the Eucharist. 'The faith of the three hundred and eighteen fathers' referred to the essentials of Nicene faith, and not necessarily to a precise text. None of the succeeding councils was held to have altered the faith of Nicaea in any way, only to have made it explicit in the face of heretical opinions.

The introduction of the creed into the Liturgy at Constantinople was a piece of ecclesiastical manoeuvring. The Macedonius to whom Theodore the Lector refers was Timothy's Chalcedonian predecessor. He had been deposed by the monophysite Emperor Anastasius I. Timothy introduced the creed which had been incorporated into the decisions of the Council of Chalcedon to demonstrate his own orthodoxy, and to disparage thereby his unfortunate predecessor. At the same time he might hope to please the Emperor by introducing into the capital a practice begun under the monophysite patronage of Peter the Fuller. The monophysites had no quarrel with the second Ecumenical Council which had produced the creed.

Despite this somewhat dubious background, the recitation of the creed secured a permanent place in the rite of Constantinople. When the bishops of the capital once more became orthodox, they could hardly remove the formula sanctioned by the Council they professed to venerate. It was a popular piece, sung by the whole congregation. There is no good reason to doubt that it was introduced in the position where it now is, though why there is not clear. In Spain in the sixth century it was inserted in the Mass before the Lord's Prayer. In Rome, when it was eventually adopted in the eleventh century, it came after the readings and sermon. Perhaps in Constantinople they did not want the catechumens to hear it until the appropriate moment in their preparation for baptism. But in whatever position it came, the basic reason for using the creed in the Eucharist was the same: it served as a test for orthodoxy in a time of doctrinal controversy. It also, in the Byzantine rite, broke the intimate liturgical link between the bringing in of the bread and wine and the prayer by which they were offered and consecrated.

The Anaphora

The creed sung, the bishop began the anaphora, usually that of Basil, less frequently that of Chrysostom. Maximus says nothing about the eucharistic prayer, except that the Sanctus is sung by the whole congregation. He gives no indication as to whether or not the prayer was still chanted out loud. We know that at the end of the eighth century most of the anaphora was said silently by the celebrant, as in present Orthodox practice. It is worth attempting to trace the origin and spread of the custom of silent recitation.

It is clear from a law of Justinian that celebrants in mid-sixth-century Constantinople and its province were beginning to recite certain prayers in both the eucharistic and baptismal liturgies in an inaudible voice. The Emperor protested vigorously and forbade the practice. His *Novella* 137 of the year 565 sought to regulate various abuses in the life of the Church, and in its last chapter prescribed as follows:

> Moreover we order all bishops and priests to say the prayers used in the divine oblation and in holy baptism not inaudibly, but in a voice that can be heard by the faithful people, that the minds of those who listen may be excited to greater compunction.

Justinian was concerned to stamp out an innovation which he rightly considered harmful to liturgical devotion. He was unsuccessful, and his failure opened the way to a fundamental change not only in liturgical practice but in popular eucharistic piety. From the latter part of the sixth century the central prayer of the Liturgy passed out of the hearing, and therefore out of the knowledge, of the great majority of Byzantine Christians who had no service books in which they could at least read what they could not hear. Few changes in the Church's worship have been so far-reaching in their implications and consequences. The principal prayer of the service became a prayer for the clergy only, for those close enough to the altar to hear it. The exclusion of the laity from the common thanksgiving and offering of the gifts powerfully reinforced the already marked clericalization of the Liturgy.

It seems that the clergy of sixth-century Constantinople were following the example of their brothers further east. The first mention of the silent recitation of prayers in the Eucharist that we have occurs in the *Liturgical Homilies* of Narsai. Narsai was a leading Nestorian teacher, who taught for twenty years in Edessa. When the followers of Ibas of Edessa, who with Theodore of Mopsuestia and Theodoret had been among the closest friends of Nestorius, were driven from Edessa, Narsai established the famous Nestorian school at Nisibis, where he remained for forty-five years until his death in 502. Narsai's description of the East Syrian Eucharist makes it clear that most of the anaphora was said by the priests inaudibly. After the introductory dialogue there was silence in the church until the priest raised his voice for the introduction to the Sanctus. The church returned to silence, while the priest began to commune with God. He raised his voice at the end of his prayer to make it audible to the people, and they concurred and acquiesced in his prayer by saying 'Amen'. The priest continued with the intercession. Narsai says nothing about inaudibility, either at this point or in his description of the invocation of the Holy Spirit, but it seems that the priest raised his voice only after the invocation, when the mysteries had been accomplished.

It was, then, in East Syria that the practice began which by the middle of the sixth century had caused the eucharistic prayer at Constantinople to become silent. It is not clear why the practice began; but it was no doubt linked with the attitude of fear and awe in the presence of the mysteries which became widespread from the middle of the fourth century, particularly in the East.

Preparation for Communion and Communion

The Lord's Prayer and the invitation to Communion, 'Holy things for holy people', followed as they had done in Chrysostom's time. By the beginning of the seventh century, however, a new custom had been introduced before the clergy received Communion. The ceremony known as the zeon consisted in pouring a little hot water into the consecrated wine. It is usually thought that the Armenian Catholicos Moses II was referring, somewhat contemptuously, to this custom when he rejected an invitation from the Emperor Maurice (582–602) to come to Constantinople for theological discussions: 'I will never cross the River Azat, nor eat bread cooked in an oven, nor drink what is warm', he is said to have replied. It was a time of controversy about the kind of bread which should be used for the Eucharist, and about the mixing of water with wine in the chalice. The Armenians had taken to using unleavened bread, and wine unmixed with water. The Byzantines saw this as a denial of the two natures in Christ, since the leaven and the water, they held, symbolized his humanity. Since the Armenians did not even mix cold water with the wine before the anaphora, they were hardly likely to approve of adding hot after. They seem to have regarded unmixed wine as symbolizing the immortality of Christ's risen life, free from the corruptibility represented by water. Leaven, too, for them was a sign of corruptibility. But for the Byzantines the use of water in the wine meant that the mysteries showed forth, as they should, the death as well as the resurrection of Christ.

It was perhaps as a complement to the addition of cold water before the consecration that hot water came to be added after: if the cold represented the death, the warm could stand for the new life of the resurrection. It has also been suggested that the background to the custom could be the teaching of the Aphthartodocetae, the extreme monophysite group towards which Justinian is sometimes thought to have leaned at the end of his life. They taught that the blood and water which flowed from the side of Christ were warm, since being God Christ did not really die. The zeon could have expressed this belief at the time of its introduction, though it was later provided with a different explanation. For several centuries no formula indicating its significance seems to have been attached to the action.

Maximus implies that lay Communion still took place, though he gives no description either of the distribution of Communion or of the conclusion of the service. Communion was no doubt accompanied by psalmic chant. It was given as it had been in the fifth century. A little later in the seventh century, the Council in Trullo of 692 found it necessary to give some explicit instructions. The clergy were not to ask for a fee for giving anyone Communion. Lay people were to receive the consecrated bread into their hands, and not into a cloth or any receptacle: 'Thus if anyone at the time of the synaxis wishes to partake of the immaculate Body and to come forward for Communion, holding his hands in the form of a cross let him come forward and receive the Communion of love.' The implication of these directives is that Communion was not a frequent practice: at any given liturgy there were many who abstained. Communion must have been distributed either, as now, in front of the holy door in the sanctuary barrier, or, in churches where the solea connected directly with the holy door without a gap, to one side or other of the door. When the Emperor communicated he did so in the sanctuary itself, his procession following the same path as it had done at the entrance of the mysteries.

Conclusion of the Service

From the year 624, in which, according to the *Chronicon Paschale*, it was introduced by the Patriarch Sergius, the hymn 'Let our mouths be filled with your praise, O Lord' was sung after Communion. The original text qualified the mysteries only as 'holy'; 'divine, immortal and lifegiving' were added later. The hymn was probably to begin with a troparion used as a refrain to the communion psalm. The prayer of thanksgiving followed, the deacon dismissed the people, and the service was over.

Towards the end of the sixth century the Patriarch Eutychius compared the end of the Liturgy with that of the Last Supper. Then, the disciples sang a hymn and went out. At the Liturgy, 'after receiving the precious Body and Blood we say a prayer of thanksgiving, and then we go out, each one to his own home'. The bishop and clergy went out, too, probably back down the solea, and so out by the route by which the mysteries had come in. The deacons carried the sacred vessels, to be returned to the skeuophylakion. There the deacons removed their stoles, the bishop his omophorion.

By the end of the eighth century, and perhaps earlier, the bishop stopped somewhere beyond the ambo to recite a final prayer, that 'said behind the ambo', in the midst of the dispersing congregation. The Liturgy had begun with a prayer as the people were about to flock into church: it finished with a prayer as they prepared to stream out of it.

The Interpretation of the Liturgy

The meaning of what is done in the Eucharist is conveyed to the worshipper in the first place by the prayers which are said during the celebration. But an understanding of the rite can grow up alongside that expressed in its text. We have seen how a symbolic interpretation of the service was given as early as the third century. The first full-scale interpretation of the Liturgy in Constantinople was provided by Maximus the Confessor in his *Mystagogia* in the first half of the seventh century. But before we look at the meaning Maximus saw in the rite, we must glance at the interpretation given over a century earlier by the so-called Dionysius the Areopagite in his treatise on *The Ecclesiastical Hierarchy*.

The writings ascribed to Dionysius – a convert of Paul's in Athens – are generally held to belong to the late fifth or early sixth century, and to come from somewhere in Northern Syria. Their real author is unknown. It is possible that they come from a background not unfavourable to monophysitism, since they are first quoted in the works of the monophysite Severus, Patriarch of Antioch 512–18. The Chalcedonians seem first to have heard them in the course of theological conversations with Severian bishops in 532. Until recently the attribution to Dionysius was generally assumed to be authentic. His writings carried therefore considerable authority. Maximus the Confessor made use of them, and so in the fifteenth century did the last of the Byzantine liturgical commentators, Symeon of Thessalonike. Dionysius' interpretation of the Eucharist must be set in the context of his whole presentation of Christianity. He drew upon the Alexandrian theological tradition, and on the philosophy of the Neoplatonists. The goal of the Christian life is union with God, whom Dionysius refers to as the One. He is the spiritual reality from whom all other spiritual realities have come, and to whom they must return. Dionysius is not afraid to speak of man's deification. But because of his disobedience man finds himself separated from God, separated from his fellows, and a prey to internal disruption. He is incapable by himself of rising above the passions which tear him apart and the material world which holds him down, and prevents him from finding his lost immortality in union with God. His mind is darkened and he cannot see where he is going.

But God, in his love for man, took on him our human nature,

sin only excepted, so that we might be united to his divine nature. Man's mind is enlightened, his soul freed from impure passions, and he is to the fullest extent possible united with God. The individual Christian must appropriate this divine gift by a process of purification and illumination, leading to union with God. He does so within the Church, whose hierarchy enables him to rise by contemplation from material realities to the spiritual realities to which they point. The real world, for Dionysius, is the spiritual world.

But we are incapable of apprehending this world directly: it is communicated to us by means of symbols. The divine mystery, which is one and spiritual, is revealed to us through what is multiple and material. So in the celebration of the sacraments the visible and tangible rites are the image of spiritual realities. From the multiplicity of the sign the human spirit can rise to the unifying vision of the One. It does so by means of contemplation, *theoria*, which is an activity of the human spirit sustained by the grace of the Holy Spirit.

To be able to contemplate the reality behind the symbol requires previous purification. That is why those who have not attained a sufficient degree of purification cannot see the Eucharist for what it most truly is, the sacrament of union with God. For them the scripture readings and psalms give instruction in the life of virtue, and in the necessity of being purified from evil. Communion for them is a reminder that they must learn to live in harmony with those with whom they have exchanged the kiss of peace. It recalls the Last Supper in which Jesus did not allow Judas to participate because he did not have the requisite purity, and so they learn that sharing in the Eucharist will only divinize them if they do so inwardly conformed to the life of Christ.

It is against this background of his general concept of the Christian life that we must understand Dionysius' interpretation of the Eucharist as above all the sacrament of union with God. He calls the rite the synaxis, a common term in early Christian usage for the Christian assembly, the gathering together of the church. But it is particularly apt for the rite as Dionysius understands it, for the Eucharist gathers us out of our separation from one another into a unity which gives us communion and union with the One. That is why, in Dionysius' view, the Eucharist is the sacrament which is the necessary complement of all the others, which without it are incomplete.

The union which the Eucharist mediates is primarily union with God. But that union is only possible when we have achieved unity within ourselves, for only those who are like God can enjoy communion with him. The Eucharist stands in sharp contrast with the sinful passions which are the cause of division within human beings and among them. The union of the individual with God entails necessarily the unity of those who enjoy communion with him among themselves.

The unifying effect of the Eucharist is symbolized at the very beginning of the rite when the bishop, having prayed in front of the altar, leaves the sanctuary in order to cense the whole assembly before returning to his place. The worshipper is to see in this the symbol of God, who while transcending all that is and remaining unchanging, comes forth in order to communicate himself to created beings and draw them into unity with himself. He is also to see in it a symbol of the Eucharist itself, which is one and indivisible, and yet, out of love for man, becomes diversified in a wealth of sacred symbols, which nevertheless return into unity, at the same time unifying all who worthily communicate. The censing, finally, symbolizes the function of the hierarch – the bishop – himself, who in his goodness towards the lower orders in the Church leaves his contemplation of the One in order to communicate his knowledge of God to them in material signs, and then returns to his contemplation, which enables him to see clearly the single reality which lies behind the manifold symbols that constitute the visible rite. All three applications of the same basic symbolism point to the love of God which condescends to man in order to raise him to the spiritual contemplation of the One.

The service continues with the readings and psalmody, from the Old Testament, the New, and, most of all, the Gospels. The psalmody, which celebrates the words and deeds of God and of godly men, prepares those who take part in its harmonious singing to receive or to administer the sacraments. It conduces the worshipper to harmony with God, within themselves, and with one another. What the psalms enunciate in brief and obscurely is expounded more fully and clearly in the readings. Because they are inspired by the one divine Spirit the Scriptures of the Old and New Testaments concur, the former predicting the works of Jesus and the latter relating them. The purpose and effect of the readings and psalmody is to prepare the worshipper for the celebration of the mysteries by drawing together those who are prepared for divinization in contemplation of the works of God.

There follow the dismissals of the catechumens, those possessed by demons, and the penitents: for they have not yet attained a purity sufficient to enable them to participate in the mysteries. The catechumens have not yet received illumination in baptism, for which they are being prepared by hearing the Scriptures. Those possessed by demons, although they have been initiated to some degree into the sacramental life of the Church, have not attained sufficient stability in their contemplation to be able to resist the attractions of the material world. Having become again a prey to distracting and corrupting passions, they too are only capable of hearing the Scriptures, which teach them to return to a better way. The penitents have already been admitted to the celebration of the mysteries. But their imperfection has prevented them from yet rising to a state of likeness with God, and therefore they too are incapable of admission to the mysteries.

After the dismissal of all those who have not yet attained a sufficiently high degree of purity, the sacred ministers and all the people sing what Dionysius calls a song of universal, or catholic, praise. It is not clear from his description of its contents what precisely this might have been. It is often thought that he is speaking of the creed, though he describes this part of the service as an act of praise for all the works of God, which have effected our union with him.

The holy bread, covered with a veil, is then presented, together with the cup of blessing, and the kiss of peace is given. The kiss unites the worshippers among themselves, and so enables them to be united with the One, for union with God is impossible for those who are divided among themselves. The diptychs of the dead are next read. They celebrate those who have achieved perfection of virtue in their life, and live now for ever united with Christ. The mention of their names in the Liturgy is a reminder to the worshippers of that union with God in perfect holiness to which we are called.

The bishop and clergy wash their hands in preparation for the most holy sacrifice; for those who approach it must be as free as possible from anything which diminishes their conformity with it. That the clergy wash their hands in the presence of the holy symbols signifies that it is only Christ who can purify us completely, and so prepare us for union with God. The bishop is united with the One in order to celebrate and distribute the sacrament of union; and in the eucharistic prayer he praises God for all he has done to unite our nature with his own.

Having celebrated the mysteries, the bishop divides and distributes the bread, and shares the chalice among all. So he mysteriously divides and distributes the unity, in which the most holy sacrifice is consummated, and to which the communicants are conformed. The act of Communion sums up in its symbolism the whole economy of our salvation. The divine Word leaves his mysterious sanctuary and descends to our lowly level because of his love for us. He unites human nature with himself without absorbing it, and so, being in his own nature one and indivisible, he shares in our fragmented nature. But he does so only so that we might share in his own life and unity with God. That demands of us a life as like his as possible, freed from corrupting passions. By reflecting on his incarnate life and following the example of his holy innocence, we shall ourselves become pure and godly, and be united with him.

So Dionysius presents the Eucharist as the sacrament *par excellence* of unity with God. It effects for those who take part in it that deifying union with the One which the incarnation has made available for the whole human race.

The *Mystagogia* of Maximus the Confessor

Maximus gave up a distinguished career in the imperial service to become a monk not far from Constantinople. The Persian invasion of 626 caused him to move to Africa, where he met the future Patriarch of Jerusalem, Sophronius. Together they were to oppose the monenergist and monothelete heresies favoured by the Emperor Heraclius and Patriarch Sergius of Constantinople. Maximus played an important part in the Lateran Council in Rome in 649, at which the doctrine of the two energies and two wills in Christ was affirmed. Because he refused to support imperial policies aimed at reconciling the monophysite communities through promoting monotheletism, he was eventually arrested, mutilated, and exiled.

Maximus was first and foremost a monk, in the tradition of Evagrius of Pontus. His defence of orthodox christological doctrine sprang as much from a spiritual as from a dogmatic concern, for he held the union of the two energies and the two wills in Christ to be a model for the union of the soul with God. His monastic spirituality was nourished by the ascetical and mystical tradition of the desert, which he integrated, in the *Mystagogia*, with the liturgical tradition of the Church. One of his great achievements was to relate Christian mysticism firmly with the mystery of Christ, from which the teaching of Evagrius and of Dionysius ran the risk of detaching it.

Maximus wrote the *Mystagogia* somewhere between 628 and 630, on his way to, or already just arrived in, Africa. It is the first of the Byzantine liturgical commentaries of which we know, and is generally assumed to be based on the rite of Constantinople. He wrote it in all probability for monks, and interprets the liturgical rite as a means of mystical ascent to union with God. He draws largely for his material on Origen, Evagrius, and Dionysius, to whose *Ecclesiastical Hierarchy* he refers twice, once to disclaim any intention of dealing with the same matters as so great a spiritual master had already treated. But he has woven the themes he has found in the tradition into an original synthesis.

By calling his work *Mystagogia* Maximus shows he intends it to lead his readers to a knowledge of the mystery of God, which though hidden can be known by revelation. The mystery is revealed in creation, in Scripture, and in the symbolism of the Liturgy, and in all three it can be apprehended by contemplation. Contemplation pierces through the symbolism of the rite to grasp the reality which is presented in the symbols, just as it perceives in nature the real meaning of created things, and discerns in Scripture the spiritual meaning contained in the letter. In all three instances contemplation is an activity of the human spirit prompted and inspired by the Holy Spirit.

In the *Mystagogia* Maximus makes frequent use of the terms figure, image and symbol to point to the presence of the mystery. These three words seem to be more or less synonymous. For Maximus, standing within the Platonic tradition, a symbol is not so much the sign of an absent reality, as the reality itself present in the symbol; and this concept lies at the root of his liturgical and sacramental symbolism. His interpretation of the Liturgy has to be set in the context of his understanding of God's plan of redemption. The figure or foreshadowing of the Old Testament is followed by the image of the New. The latter points to the reality to be realized at the end of time. The incarnation of the Word is the source of man's divinization in all these stages, present with increasing intensity in each successive phase of the divine economy.

Maximus is the first commentator to give an interpretation of the church building as well as of the Liturgy which is celebrated in it. He makes no use of the potential symbolic value of the dome, although he gives no fewer than five interpretations of the church's significance.

First, the Church – that composed of souls rather than of stones – is an image of God himself, since it gathers into one the different men, women and children to whom it has given new birth by the Holy Spirit. All form one body in Christ, all are of one heart and one soul within the Church, in whose fellowship all the characteristics which distinguish and separate people from one another are transcended. In the same way God unites all that exists in his creation, binding them together among themselves by uniting them with himself.

The church made of stones, which for Maximus is a kind of icon of the Church composed of people, is from another point of view an image of the world, which is made up of things visible and invisible. The sanctuary, reserved for the priests and ministers, represents the invisible, spiritual universe; the nave, reserved for the faithful people, represents the visible, material creation – though both are inseparably united. The nave is potentially the sanctuary, the sanctuary is the nave in action. The church made by hands reveals that not made by hands, the created universe, which is a kind of church.

The church is also an image of the visible, tangible world: for the sky it has the sanctuary, for the earth, the beauty of the nave. Conversely, the world is a church, whose sanctuary is the sky and whose nave the earth.

It represents man, too, and is his image and likeness, as he is created in God's. The nave symbolizes his body, and the acquisition of a virtuous life. The sanctuary is his soul, giving to his contemplation of nature a spiritual interpretation. The holy altar is his spirit, penetrating into the mystical knowledge of God. Conversely, man can be considered a mystical church.

But the church is also the image of the soul by itself. The sanctuary represents man's spirit, the principle of the contemplative life; the nave represents his reason, principle of the active life. The sanctuary points to the ascent of man's spirit, which by contemplation arrives at knowledge of the truth. The nave points to the elevation of his reason, which by practice of the virtues attains to the good. The fruit of the active and contemplative life together is the soul's divinization, which is symbolized by the mystery celebrated on the holy altar.

So the church is the symbol both of God's condescension in love for man and of man's attempt to find God. In it the mystery and mysticism meet, to effect man's divinization in union with God. It is an icon of the Church not made with hands, but composed of people: an icon too of the Church which is eternal, in the heavens. For although there is an inseparable unity between visible and invisible, material and spiritual, in the world, in man and in the Church, nevertheless the visible and material is destined to die in order to be raised to a new and glorious existence, in which it will have become like that which is invisible and spiritual.

Of the Liturgy itself Maximus gives a twofold explanation. First, it represents the whole history of God's saving plan, from the incarnation to the second coming of Christ. The entry of the bishop into the church is the figure of the first coming of Christ in the flesh. By his incarnate life Christ frees human nature from the corruption and mortality into which it had fallen by sin. Having given himself as a ransom for us in his life-giving passion, he led us back into the grace of his Kingdom. Then he ascended into heaven and reoccupied his heavenly throne, of which the bishop's entry into the sanctuary and ascent to his throne are the figures.

The entry of the people signifies the passage of those who believe from ignorance and error to the knowledge of God, as well as their passage from evil and ignorance to virtue and knowledge. It symbolizes every act of repentance and return to the life of virtue. The readings of the Old and New Testaments instruct us in God's purposes, and show us how we are to wage the spiritual warfare to which we are called. The psalms signify the joy which reveals the good things of God, and which moves us to hatred of sin and pure love for God. The bishop's greeting, 'Peace be with you', before each reading represents the favours dispensed by the angels, to assist us in the struggle against evil, and to give us peace and freedom from the passions as the fruit of our acquisition of virtue.

The proclamation of the Gospel signifies the end of the world. The descent of the bishop from his throne symbolizes the second coming of Christ to judge the world, and to separate the just from the unjust, giving to each the recompense his life has deserved. The closing of the church doors and the dismissal of the cate-chumens signifies the folding-up of the material order, and the entry of those who are worthy into the spiritual world, the bridal chamber of Christ.

'The entry of the holy and venerable mysteries' is the beginning of the new teaching there will be in heaven about God's purpose for us: it is the revelation of the mystery of our salvation hidden in God. The kiss of peace represents the harmony and concord that will bind all together in the world to come, when those who are worthy of it will enjoy an intimate union with the Word of God. The creed symbolizes the eternal thanksgiving to God for all his providence towards us, while the Sanctus in the anaphora represents our future union with the bodiless spiritual powers of heaven.

Maximus passes over the rest of the eucharistic prayer, to interpret the Lord's Prayer as the sign of our adoption as true sons of God, which we shall receive by the gift and grace of the Holy Spirit. The people's acclamation 'One is holy, etc.' at the end of the mystic ceremony represents the gathering of all who have been initiated into God, and their union with God, one and simple, whose glory they will contemplate, sharing the purity of the angels. Finally, Communion both points to, and in part realizes, man's divinization in the world to come:

> Afterwards, as the climax of everything, comes the distribution of the sacrament which transforms into itself and renders similar to the causal good by grace and participation those who worthily share in it. To them is there lacking nothing of this good that is possible and attainable for men, so that they can be and be called gods by adoption through grace because all of God entirely fills them and leaves no part of them empty of his presence (Maximus Confessor, *Selected Writings*, p. 203).

As well as this general significance the Liturgy has a special significance, according to which the Eucharist symbolizes the mystical ascent of the soul to God. Maximus therefore goes on 'to consider and perceive how the divine precepts of holy Church lead the soul, by a true and active knowledge, to its own perfection'. His exposition in chapter twenty-three is concise, and we can follow it largely in his own words.

Maximus invites 'the genuine lover of Christ's blessed wisdom' to see in the entry into the church the soul's flight from 'the outside error and confusion of material things' and their warring, destructive appearances 'to an inviolable shelter of peace in the natural contemplation in the Spirit', and to consider how free of any fighting or disorder it enters (the church) together with reason and before the Word and our great and true High Priest of God. There it learns, by symbols of the divine readings which take place, the principles of beings and the marvellous and grand mysteries of divine Providence revealed in the Law and the Prophets, and it receives in each, by the beautiful instruction divinely given in them through the holy angels who spiritually communicate to it the true understanding, the peaceful meanings with the strengthening and preserving enchantment of the divine and ardent desire for God by means of the spiritual appeal of the divine chants singing in it mystically. And consider again how the soul passes beyond this and concentrates on the one and only summit, the holy Gospel, which collects these principles together into one and in which pre-exist in one form all the principles both of Providence and of existing things in a single burst of meaning. Following this, it is permitted to those who love God to see by a divine perception with the undaunted eyes of the mind the Word of God come to it from heaven and symbolized by the bishop's descent from his priestly throne. He separates as catechumens the thoughts which are still formed from the senses and divisible because of them from its perfect part. And thence again it leaves the world of sense as suggested by the closing of the doors of God's holy church, and leads it to the understanding of immaterial things signified by the entrance into the unutterable mysteries, an understanding which is immaterial, simple, immutable, divine, free of all form and shape, and by which the soul gathers to itself its proper powers and comes face to face with the Word, having united by a spiritual kiss both the principles and ineffable modes of its own salvation and teaching through the symbol of faith to confess this with thanksgiving.

From this moment on the soul is rendered as far as possible simple and indivisible by its instruction, having encompassed by knowledge the principles of both sensible and intelligible things. The Word then leads it to the knowledge of theology made manifest after its journey through all things, granting it an understanding equal to the angels as far as possible for it. He will teach it with such wisdom that it will comprehend the one God, one nature and three Persons, unity of essence in three persons and consubstantial trinity of persons; trinity in unity and unity in trinity; not one and the other, or one without the other, or one through the other, or one in the other, or one from the other, but the same in itself and by itself and next to itself, the same with itself ... one, single, undivided, unconfused, simple, undiminished, and unchangeable divinity, completely one in essence and completely three in persons, and sole ray shining in the single form of one triple-splendoured light. In this light the soul now equal in dignity with the holy angels, having received the luminous principles which are accessible to creation in regard to divinity and having learned to praise in concert with them without keeping silent the one Godhead in a triple cry, is brought to the adoption of similar likeness by grace. By this, in having God through prayer as its mystical and only Father by grace, the soul will centre on the oneness of his hidden being by a distraction from all things, and it will experience or rather know divine things all the more as it does not want to be its own nor able to be recognized from or by itself or anyone else's but only all of God's who takes it up becomingly and fittingly as only he can, penetrating it completely without passion and deifying all of it and transforming it unchangeably to himself (ibid. pp. 204–6).

So the salvation which God has made available to all by the incarnation and passion of the Word is made available to individual Christians according to their capacity to receive it. No wonder that Maximus exhorts all to be in regular attendance at church, and never to miss the holy synaxis which is celebrated there

because of the holy angels who remain there and who take note each time people enter and present themselves to God, and they make supplications for them; likewise because of the grace of the Holy Spirit which is always invisibly present, but in a special way at the time of the holy synaxis. This grace transforms and changes each person who is found there and in fact remoulds him in proportion to what is more divine in him and leads him to what is revealed through the mysteries which are celebrated, even if he does not himself feel this because he is still among those who are children in Christ, unable to see either into the depths of the reality or the grace operating in it, which is revealed through each of the divine symbols of salvation being accomplished, and which proceeds according to the order and progression from preliminaries to the end of everything (ibid. pp. 206f.).

The *Mystagogia* of Maximus the Confessor seems to have had a fairly wide readership, to judge from the number of manuscript copies which have survived, though it probably never attained the popularity of some of the later commentaries. It had a special appeal for those living the monastic life, who could appreciate the mystical interpretation of the Liturgy. But as the first Byzantine work of its kind, it helped to establish a tradition, and to popularize a way of understanding and living the Liturgy which became an accepted part of Orthodox Christianity.

6 The Liturgy after the Victory of the Icons

The Liturgy in the early seventh century still preserved its early simplicity of structure, although to the actions and prayers which made up the primary core of the rite secondary elements had already been added. When evidence for the text of the Liturgy first emerges in the Codex Barberini of the late eighth or early ninth century it is clear that subsequent developments have begun the process by which the primary elements became increasingly surrounded, and to some extent obscured, by additions to the service.

The eighth century was a turning-point in the development of Byzantine worship. It witnessed the controversy over the veneration of icons, whose vindication opened the way for the formulation of a scheme of church decoration which linked the sacred building and its iconography closely with the celebration of the Liturgy. The Liturgy itself came to be understood as a kind of icon, and it was in this period that the foundation of its subsequent interpretation was laid by the *Ecclesiastical History* of Germanos, Patriarch of Constantinople (died 733), one of our chief sources of information for the Liturgy in the eighth and ninth centuries.

The Iconoclastic Controversy

We have seen that the Byzantine tradition of religious art drew upon both the naturalistic Hellenistic tradition, and that of Mesopotamia, with its fully-frontal representation of holy persons in such a way as to emphasize their presence to the beholder. This technique had been increasingly used in Byzantine religious art in the sixth and seventh centuries, not only in the decoration of churches, but in the making of portable icons, kept and venerated at home. The earliest portable icons to have survived, from the late sixth or early seventh centuries, are remarkably similar to those produced after the theology of icons had been fully worked out in the course of the iconoclastic controversy.

Such images came to be honoured by lighting candles in front of them and burning incense before them, in the same way as Christians in the fourth century had venerated the image of Constantine.

The veneration of icons had no doubt sometimes been exaggerated in popular religious devotion but the attack launched against icons in the early eighth century was directed against any use of images in a religious context. It began in Asia Minor, and found powerful imperial patronage in Leo III, who had been commander of the army in Asia before becoming Emperor in 717. In 726 the famous icon of Christ over the Chalke Gate of the imperial palace in Constantinople was destroyed. Popular disturbances resulted, and the government took action against the defenders of the images. Persecution continued under Leo's successor, Constantine V (741–75).

From Syria St John of Damascus defended the making and veneration of icons. Denying the charge of idolatry, he distinguished clearly between the worship due to God and the veneration paid to images of Christ and the saints. The second commandment had to be understood in the light of the circumstances in which it was framed. Even in Judaism representations of living creatures were allowed. For Christians the incarnation of the Son of God was the primary justification for making representations: if God had taken human flesh, then the incarnate Lord could be represented pictorially.

The iconoclasts argued that the only permissible figure of the humanity of Christ was the bread and wine of the Eucharist. They pointed out that the Fathers of the Church had left behind no prayer for the hallowing images. Painted representations implied heresy: either the painter confuses the manhood with the Godhead, and so falls into monophysitism; or he represents the manhood alone, and so like Nestorius separates it from the divinity. Iconoclast doctrine was embodied in the decisions of the Council of Hieria in 754. Meanwhile images were removed from churches, and the use of portable icons banned. Only symbolic art might be used in decorating churches, and the cross became a frequent feature of iconoclast art. There was no objection to the representation of animals or birds, of plants or trees.

Opposition to iconoclasm was centred in the monastic communities. The controversy evoked fierce passions, and there were extremists on both sides. Persecution of iconodules continued until Leo IV's accession in 775. Under his widow Irene a moderate iconodule Tarasius became patriarch, and in 787 the Seventh Ecumenical Council of Nicaea met and drew up a definition of Orthodox belief about icons and their veneration, based on the teaching of St John of Damascus. The Council repudiated the iconoclasts' claim that the consecrated elements in the Eucharist were the only permissible icon of Christ: they are no icon, but the very reality of his Body and Blood, identical with him in essence. It affirmed that the veneration given to icons is distinct from the worship due to God, and is paid rather to their prototypes, for the image is identical with its prototype according to its meaning, even though it differs from it according to its essence. Images, whether painted on wood or made of mosaic or fresco, can rightly be honoured with candles and incense, and a hierarchy is to be discerned among them: the icon of Christ comes first, then that of his Mother. Next come images of the angels who have appeared in embodied form, and then those of apostles, martyrs and other saints.

Iconoclasm revived in the early part of the ninth century, and it was not until 843 that Theodora, widow of the last iconoclast Emperor Theophilus, working with the moderate iconodule Patriarch Methodius, reaffirmed the decisions of the Council of 787. The controversy had so integrated the veneration of icons into Orthodox practice, and so closely linked its justification with the doctrine of the incarnation, that the final restoration of the icons came to be celebrated on the first Sunday of Lent as the Victory of Orthodoxy. At the beginning of the controversy the defenders of icons emphasized their educational and evangelical value: images represent pictorially what the Scriptures describe in words. By the end of the controversy there was far greater stress on their sacramental character as making present to the worshipper what they represented. Icons had come to be seen as a means of grace, enabling the worshipper to stand in faith before the person depicted and to converse with him or her.

Church Design and Decoration in the Ninth Century

Three basic principles of church decoration governed the development of iconography after the victory of the icons. The image must first be made so as to make clear its identity of meaning with its prototype: persons and events must be clearly recognizable. Not only were they depicted in accordance with fixed rules, but they were identified by a title. This enabled the worshipper to

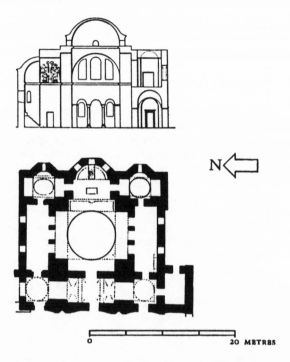

The church of the Dormition at Nicaea, early eighth century, showing the plan and section of an early cross-domed church.

relate to the image, which had further to be represented frontally, so that there could be a real meeting between the image and its prototype, and the beholder. The worshipper really stood before Christ, his Mother and the saints: he was present at the nativity, the crucifixion, the resurrection and the ascension. Finally, each image had to occupy its proper place in the hierarchical order of things: first Christ, then his Mother, then the angels and saints in their due order of precedence.

The pattern of church decoration that embodied these principles was, from the ninth century onwards, normally applied to a church designed as a cross within a square, surmounted by a central cupola. The variety of shapes which had been used in previous centuries gave way to the shape which embodied as completely as possible the Byzantine concept of the church

106

building as itself a symbolic space, and which provided the best possible framework for the hierarchical arrangement of the images it needed to contain. From this time on it is less than adequate to speak of church decoration, for the mosaics or frescoes applied to the building formed an integral part of the sacred space into which the worshipper entered for the celebration of the sacred mysteries. Church building, church decoration and the Liturgy coalesced into a complex of symbols, in which the divine mystery of God's saving love was made present in order that the worshipper might be caught up into it and participate in the worship and life of heaven.

The first church of which we have a description in the immediate post-iconoclastic period is the New Church, built in the imperial palace in Constantinople by the Emperor Basil I, and dedicated in honour of the Mother of God. It was perhaps cautious in its use of images, for it made use only of individual figures, not of representations of events: icons had been defended first of all as a means of communication with persons. Preaching at its consecration in 881 Patriarch Photius said:

> In the dome there is a figure of a man, representing Christ, made of small coloured stones. You could say that he is looking down over the world, and considering its order and its government, so strikingly has the artist expressed, in shape and colour, the Creator's providence for us. In the cross-shaped sections around the dome of the cupola a large number of angels is depicted, who crowd around their Lord to serve him. From the apse which rises from the sanctuary there shines forth the figure of the Virgin, who spreads out her immaculate hands for us, and bestows on the Emperor good fortune and victory over his enemies. The apostles and martyrs, and the prophets and patriarchs, adorn the temple, which is filled with their images.

Worshippers, entering such a church, entered an image of the universe. In the dome, symbolizing heaven, from which light streamed down, they saw Christ Pantocrator, ruling the universe he had created and redeemed. In the highest vaults around the dome they saw the heavenly hosts of angels. In the conch of the apse, the next highest space, they saw the Mother of God, symbol of the Church. From the upper parts of the walls, in their due order, the saints confronted them. They themselves, though still on earth, in the lowest part of the church, yet knew and could see that here and now they had fellowship with the saints and angels, and dared even to claim their part in the life of the glorified Christ, in whom they could hope to share in the hidden yet mysteriously revealed life of the Holy Trinity. For they had entered a church which was not only a visual proclamation of the gospel, but an icon of that salvation which it made available for their appropriation.

The Liturgy in the Ninth Century

This is the earliest period for which we have definite knowledge of the text of the Liturgy in the Byzantine Church. The Codex Barberini dates from about AD 800, and contains the prayers used by the celebrant at the different services of the Church. So far as the Liturgy is concerned, this euchologion contains the prayers that make up the rite of St Basil, which is explicitly ascribed to him, and which is given first. At this time it was still the Liturgy most frequently used. The prayers of a second rite are given, except where they are identical with those of the first rite. They make up what came to be known as the Liturgy of St John Chrysostom, although in the Codex only some of the prayers are explicitly ascribed to him. In both rites there is a considerable number of prayers and formulae which certainly do not go back to the late fourth and early fifth centuries, though as we have seen it is possible that the earliest stratum in each rite owes its present form to its respective traditional author. The deacon's prayers are not included in the rite, although they are sometimes indicated, and there is only a minimum of rubrical direction. The euchologion gives the skeleton of the rite, which must be clothed and animated from other sources of information. The chief of these is the commentary on the Liturgy written by Germanos I, Patriarch of Constantinople 715–30, called *Ecclesiastical History and Mystical Contemplation*. Its popularity as an interpretation of the Liturgy caused it to be added to as time went on, to match developments in the rite itself. Consequently the *Ecclesiastical History* in its different recensions is a valuable witness to the shape of the Liturgy at several stages in its growth.

The Codex Barberini shows that several developments had taken place since the seventh century, which are of considerable importance for the shape of the Liturgy. Additions had been made to the rite which tended to obscure the clear structure it still had in the time of Maximus, and some of these were to develop

still further in the next few centuries. Three of the most significant additions had been made at the beginning of the Liturgy.

The Prothesis

The first was, strictly speaking, less an addition to the service
itself than one to the preliminary preparation of the elements. We
have seen how in the East the people deposited their offerings of
bread and wine on their way into church, and how, at the Great
Church at any rate, they did so at the skeuophylakion, detached
from the church itself. From these sufficient was set aside for the
Liturgy. No mention is made of what to begin with was a purely
practical action until the early eighth century, when Germanos
shows that it had acquired symbolic significance. The bread of
the prothesis was taken and pierced by a liturgical spear. This
may have been done in silence in Germanos' time. But by the
time of the Codex Barberini the prayer of oblation in the present
rite of the prothesis had been added in the rite of St Basil, to be
said by the priest in the skeuophylakion while he puts the bread
onto the paten.

In the middle of the ninth century the first elaboration of this
part of the rite had taken place. The version of Germanos'
explanation translated by Anastasius the Librarian in 869–70
contained an additional paragraph describing a more complex
prothesis rite than that of Germanos himself:

> The priest receives the prosphora on a paten from the deacon
> or subdeacon, takes the lance and cleans it, then makes the sign
> of the cross on the prosphora with it and says 'He was led as a
> sheep to the slaughter, and as a sheep before his shearer is
> dumb.' When he has said this he puts the prosphora on the
> holy paten and pointing to it says: 'So he opened not his mouth:
> in his humility his judgement was taken away, his generation
> who can tell? For his life is removed from the earth.' Having
> said this he takes the holy chalice and the deacon, pouring into
> it wine and water, says: 'There came out of his side water and
> blood, and he who saw it bears witness and his witness is true.'
> And after this putting the holy chalice on the holy table he
> points to the sacrificial lamb represented by the bread, and the
> blood shed represented by the wine, looks intently at them and
> says: 'There are three that bear witness, the Spirit and the
> water and the blood, and the three are one. Now and always

and for ever.' Then he takes the censer and when he has censed them he says the prayer of the prothesis.

The significance of the bread and the incision made in it in the original version of the *Ecclesiastical History*, in which Germanos refers to Isaiah 53.7 and John 19.34 without indicating whether or not they were spoken, has given rise a century later to liturgical formulae making that significance explicit. The development of the prothesis has meant that it is now performed by the priest, and has ceased to be part of the deacon's liturgy.

It has often been said that this formal preparation of the gifts must have been performed originally just before they were brought in at the Great Entrance. This supposition has been made partly because other rites have an offertory prayer at that point – the Byzantine prayer of prothesis is found in the Liturgy of St James in connection with the Great Entrance – and partly because Germanos speaks of the proskomidia at that moment in his explanation of the Liturgy as well as at the beginning. But it is equally likely that the prayer of prothesis was borrowed from the Byzantine rite by the Liturgy of St James and that Germanos speaks of the proskomidia just before the Great Entrance because originally the preliminary prothesis concerned only the bread, while the mixing of the chalice was done just before the deacons brought in the gifts. The likelihood is that the prothesis rite did not exist at all until some time between Maximus and Germanos, and that when it appeared it was as the ritualized form of the preliminary preparation of the bread in the skeuophylakion: it was never transferred to that position from elsewhere in the Liturgy.

The prayer of oblation which soon came to be recited at it anticipates the function of the anaphora by asking God to accept the gifts at the heavenly altar before the Liturgy has even begun. Its introduction must have both reflected and reinforced the tendency to think of the gifts as somehow already holy by the time the Liturgy begins. What began as a simple, even if significant, ceremony, was destined to flourish exceedingly in the coming centuries.

The Antiphons

The second significant addition made to the rite by the end of the eighth century were the three antiphons. Germanos mentions them at the beginning of the century. The three accompanying prayers provided in the Codex Barberini are found in the Liturgy today.

The antiphons were psalms or portions of psalms chanted with a refrain between verses. In the ninth and tenth centuries they were usually Psalms 91 (92), 92 (93) and 94 (95). In Constantinople the usual refrains were: 'At the prayers of the Mother of God, Saviour, save us'; 'Alleluia'; and 'Only-begotten Son', a composition attributed to Justinian. The latter was sometimes transferred to the second antiphon if the third was provided with a special refrain for a festival.

The origin of this addition to the Liturgy seems to have been the custom of singing three antiphons as a separate short service in the course of the processions which took place on certain occasions before the Liturgy, when the patriarch went formally from the Great Church to the church where the Liturgy was to be celebrated. Certainly in the tenth century these processional antiphons were considered the equivalent of the usual three at the beginning of the Liturgy, and when the procession arrived at the stational church the Liturgy began with the Trisagion. The custom no doubt antedates the tenth century.

There was already, as we have seen, an entry chant at the beginning of the Liturgy, consisting of a psalm with a refrain, or troparion, which at one time was the Trisagion. To this single entry psalm were added, some time between the early seventh and early eighth centuries, two further psalms, in order to make normal practice conform to the special practice of the stational processions. The nearest suitable psalms in the psalter seem to have been added to the existing entry psalm. This was usually Psalm 94 (95), suited by reason of the verse 'Let us come before his presence with thanksgiving'. Psalm 93 (94) was too bloodthirsty, and was passed over in favour of 91 (92) and 92 (93).

The troparion, 'Only-begotten Son', was probably already attached to Psalm 94 (95) when it stood by itself as the entrance psalm as the refrain for most Sundays. It had presumably at some stage displaced the Trisagion, which nevertheless kept a place in the Liturgy, shorn of the psalm it had once accompanied, only its manner of execution hinting at its former function.

It is not clear whether the prayers of the antiphons were recited out loud or silently. Perhaps they were at one time said out loud, preceded by the deacon's invitation, 'Let us pray to the Lord'. The so-called Lesser Litany, which from the tenth century was said before the second and third antiphons, may in origin be simply an amplification of this bidding, designed to accompany the prayer once it came to be said silently.

The three antiphons were not regarded as a fixed part of the Liturgy for several centuries. They could be omitted when there was a procession to a stational church, whether or not antiphons were sung during it; and up to the twelfth century in Constantinople the patriarch made his entry only during the third antiphon. But their introduction had important consequences, for it meant that the service no longer began with the entry of the clergy, let alone with that of the people. By this time, it seems, they gathered in the church before the Liturgy began. It was only the clergy who entered formally, and that only after the service had begun. While it is true that in the large and well-staffed churches of the capital the bishop made his entrance only during the third antiphon, Germanos early in the eighth century could already refer at this point to the entry of the Gospel. The book of Gospels had for centuries been carried in the entry procession. But now it is coming to be regarded as the chief feature of the entry.

In churches which were not provided with separate external skeuophylakia the entry was still further changed in its form and significance. In the post-iconoclastic period churches were commonly built with two side apses flanking the larger sanctuary apse. The northern came to be used for the prothesis, and was so called, the southern for the storage of vestments, books, and other liturgical equipment. In such churches the preparation of the bread and wine, now required to be done by a priest, was no doubt, in its simplest form, performed during the first two antiphons. The entry of the clergy with the Gospels became simply a procession from the chapel of the prothesis to the sanctuary, passing through the church. The real entrance of Maximus' time was becoming the so-called 'Little Entrance' of the Byzantine Liturgy in its final form. This transformation had begun by the ninth century, if not in the city itself, at any rate in the provinces. The entry prayer thus came to be attached to the entry into the sanctuary instead of the entry into the church. Perhaps the prayer of the entry in Codex Barberini's second rite, which alone survived into the present Orthodox Liturgy, reflects this situation, since its reference to the entry of the angels better fits the entry of the clergy into the sanctuary than that of people into the church.

The Great Litany

At some time during the ninth century it became the custom to recite the synapte, or litany, after the entry and before the Trisagion. Its original position was after the readings and homily, and the dismissal of the catechumens – the place where the great intercession, or prayers of the faithful, had always been. So firmly for a while did it make its home after the entry that in the tenth century it was sometimes referred to as the synapte of the Trisagion, and the prayer of the Trisagion was said silently by the priest while the deacon was chanting the petitions of the litany. The synapte did not lose its original place, however: it continued to be recited, in full or in an abridged form, in its old position. Placed after the entry, the synapte further complicated the beginning of the service, and separated the Trisagion from the entry to which it had once belonged.

The Readings

In the seventh century the Byzantine rite still had three readings, from the Old and New Testaments and the Gospels. By Germanos' time the Old Testament reading had disappeared. It left behind the psalm which had been sung between the first two readings. It came to be called the prokeimenon, a term which in the usage of Constantinople referred to a psalm verse sung before a psalm itself, whose final clause only was repeated after each verse of the psalm as a refrain. For centuries all or a large part of the psalm was so sung: it was only much later that the psalmody here, as in other places, suffered drastic reduction.

The Litany of Fervent Supplication

In the Codex Barberini the readings are followed by a litany called ektene, from the adjective meaning fervent or insistent and applied here to intercession or supplication. The litany of fervent supplication differs from the synapte in several respects. Its petitions are addressed to God himself, and are not requests for the people's prayers. Its opening petitions contain three verbs of asking, and the response, for most of the petitions, is a triple Kyrie eleison.

In the ninth century and later this litany varied a good deal in its content and in the detail of its structure. It seems to have begun by the deacon indicating to the people the response: 'Let us say Kyrie eleison', and then urging them to pray in the right spirit: 'With all our soul and with all our mind let us say'. The petitions forming the core of the litany had an emphatically penitential character, as did the priest's prayer. The original final petition, 'Have mercy on us O God according to your great mercy' was based on Psalm 51 (50): to it the people responded with a variable number of Kyrie eleisons, sometimes specified as nine or twelve. The response to the other petitions was a single Kyrie eleison, and it was the final response that gave the litany its name.

Its origin is to be sought in the penitential processions of supplication, or rogations, which were held in the capital on the anniversaries of natural or other disasters from which Constantinople suffered. Each time the procession halted the deacon recited the ektene, or 'great Kyrie eleison'. On certain occasions the station included scripture readings, and it was after the Gospel that the ektene was used. It was no doubt in imitation of this practice that the ektene was introduced into the Liturgy, at about the same time as the synapte was moved to its new position after the entry. The Codex Barberini shows that it was introduced before the end of the eighth century.

The effect of this addition was to obscure the structure of the rite at this point. The prayers of the faithful, offered in the petitions of the synapte, had earlier always followed the dismissal of the catechumens, since they were not considered capable of praying with the faithful, having not yet received the Spirit in baptism. By the eighth century the dismissal of the catechumens was a meaningless survival, and no one saw any incongruity in inserting prayers offered by the faithful before it.

The Prayers of the Faithful

The Codex Barberini contains two prayers, called the prayers of the faithful, said after the dismissal of the catechumens. The first is said 'after the eileton (corporal) has been unfolded'. The prayers for the two rites are those found in the modern Liturgy.

The prayers given for the Liturgy of St Basil have little to do with the faithful. They are prayers of the clergy and for the clergy, and both are prayers of preparation for the celebration of the Eucharist. They have no connection with the original prayers of the faithful, and reflect a later stage in the understanding of the role of the clergy in the service and their relationship with the laity.

The prayers given for the second rite are also concerned with the clergy, the first exclusively so, the second partly with them, partly with the laity. They reflect the tendency, which had been growing since the fourth century, of distinguishing the clergy from the laity not only physically, in the arrangements of the church, but spiritually. The clergy were closer to the altar not only because their place was in the sanctuary, but because of the ministry committed to them at their ordination. In all these prayers the 'we' refers to the clergy alone – a complete contrast with the older prayers in the Liturgy in which the 'we' is spoken by the bishop as the tongue of the whole people of God. The people have now become 'those who pray with us', and whose prayers are offered to God by the clergy. There could hardly be a greater contrast with Chrysostom's insistence that the prayers of the faithful – in the original sense of that term – were one of the moments in the Eucharist when there is no distinction between clergy and laity.

Behind this development lay the comparison commonly made from the fourth century onwards between the ministry of the Church of the New Covenant with that of the Church of the Old. Only the High Priest in the old dispensation was able to enter the holy of holies, to offer sacrifices of propitiation for the people. The implications of this view for the Christian priesthood were reinforced from the end of the fifth century by the teaching of Dionysius the Areopagite. For him the whole universe is hierarchically organized. Beneath the celestial hierarchy is the ecclesiastical, each of whose orders mediates to those below the illumination which comes from God, enabling those below to be purified and illuminated, and so gradually to ascend to the knowledge and contemplation of God. Dionysius' ideas had wide currency, and strengthened the earlier tendency to make of the clergy a distinct class, set apart from the rest of the Church, and possessing a mediatorial role between the laity and God.

In the celebration of the Liturgy this process was both reflected and strengthened by the spreading custom of reciting most of the prayers of the service inaudibly. Justinian's attempt to combat its establishment in Constantinople failed, and by the end of the eighth century it was well established. The Codex Barberini indicates that certain of the prayers are to be read 'mystically' by the priest. They include most of the anaphora after the Sanctus, though not, it seems, the first part of the prayer. Some prayers not so marked would certainly have been said silently as well. Prayers such as prayers of the faithful, which are purely clerical devotions, were never intended to be said out loud. It is impossible to be certain which prayers were still recited audibly in the ninth century. The rubric 'out loud' which precedes the final doxology of all the prayers in the Codex Barberini does not necessarily imply that the prayers themselves were said silently. It is found, for example, before the doxology of the Lord's Prayer, which was sung by the people. It may simply indicate that the doxology was to be sung in a more solemn manner. In the anaphora those parts which are said 'mystically' conclude with a final phrase chanted 'out loud' which leads into the people's response.

In more recent Orthodox practice the two prayers of the faithful are accompanied by two short litanies. Before the twelfth century the second was a more or less complete version of the synapte. It tended to be shortened because the whole synapte was now recited earlier on. In some churches a few of the petitions of the synapte still form part of the second litany. Underlying this rather puzzling form is the original great synapte, the real prayers of the faithful. Their former presence is indicated by the introduction to the first of the two existing short litanies: 'Let us who are believers ... in peace pray to the Lord', with which the prayers of the faithful began in the Clementine Liturgy. In the old Constantinopolitan tradition the one litany was accompanied by two prayers, one recited silently by the priest while the deacon sang the biddings, the other said by him out loud as the concluding prayer of the litany. In the first the priest asked for grace to be able to offer to God the prayers of the people, in the second he invoked God's blessing on them and asked for their worthy participation in the mysteries about to be celebrated. The litany was perhaps divided into two when the original function of the two prayers was no longer understood, and when both had come to be recited inaudibly.

The Great Entrance

The Codex Barberini provides a prayer to be said by the priest for himself while the Cherubic Hymn is being sung. It is given only for the Liturgy of St Basil, though it may well have been used in the second rite, and its text is close to that of the modern rite. One variant is of interest. The prayer speaks of Christ as the one who 'offers and is offered, sanctifies and is sanctified'. The text which eventually prevailed out of a number of alternatives read: 'who offers and is offered, receives and is distributed'. In the twelfth century a theological controversy centred on these words. If Christ is the person of the Trinity who offers the Eucharist, can he be said also to receive it? Two councils held in Constantinople in 1156 and 1157 decided that the eucharistic sacrifice was offered by Christ to the Holy Trinity, to the Father and to the Holy Spirit as well as to himself. The prayer of the Cherubic Hymn is another private prayer of the priest of the kind called 'apologies', and is the only one in the Liturgy couched in the first person singular – something quite foreign to the classical liturgical tradition of the Church. That, and its address to Christ, mark it as a comparatively late composition. Its content is in essence similar to that of the prayers of the faithful and the prayer of the proskomidia, which is the original Byzantine prayer of preparation for the celebration of the mysteries.

It was several centuries before the prayer acquired its present place in the complex of actions and prayers accompanying the bringing in of the gifts and their placing on the altar. Meanwhile its precise position varied. So long as the bishop or priest took no part in the procession, it could be said, as the Codex Barberini implies, while the procession was coming in. It eventually settled down before the entrance of the mysteries and was begun when the choir began the Cherubic Hymn.

Early in the eighth century Germanos mentions the proskomidia immediately before the entry of the gifts. As we have seen, it is unlikely that he is referring to more than the immediate preparation of the chalice. Like the prothesis before the Liturgy began, concerned with the preparation of the bread, it took place in the skeuophylakion at the Great Church. The gifts were brought in by the deacons, escorted by candles, incense and liturgical fans. The bishop received them in the sanctuary, set them on the altar, and when he had covered them with a veil, censed them. He then said the prayer of the proskomidia.

The Kiss of Peace and the Creed

In the ninth century, and for some time after, the kiss of peace was still exchanged by the whole congregation after the completion of the Great Entrance. No doubt the ancient custom was maintained of exchanging the kiss within certain groups, clergy with clergy, men with men, women with women. The orderly character of the ceremony emerges clearly from a tenth-century description in the *De Ceremoniis* of the Emperor's part in the exchange on an occasion when he participated formally in the Liturgy:

> The sovereigns go out again (from the imperial box, or meta-torion) for the kiss of peace, and the Patriarch stands within the chancel on the right side of the sanctuary, towards the metator-ion, and the sovereigns, standing outside the chancel, give the kiss first of all to the Patriarch, then after him to the syncellos and all the metropolitans and archbishops, and to the proto-pope of the Great Church, and to the dignitaries of the Patriarch. All those who give the kiss of peace to the Emperors the referendarius leads up by the hand. Then the Emperors give the kiss of peace to the Patriarch again, then going down a little from the chancel they give the kiss of peace to all those of the senate, all of whom the master of ceremonies leads up by the hand. And after greeting the Patriarch the sovereigns depart for the metatorion (cf. Taft, op. cit., p. 396).

The kiss of peace was still a significant part of the service.

When it had been concluded the deacon proclaimed 'The doors, the doors'. In the Codex Barberini it is no doubt a relic of the time when the doors of the church were closed after the dismissal of the catechumens. We have seen that this was still done in the early seventh century. The doors should of course have been closed before the entry of the mysteries, though one set of doors would have had to be opened for the procession so long as it came from outside the church itself. But a final warning may have been felt to be in place before the anaphora began. There is a similar duplication in the Clementine Liturgy of the warning to catechumens to depart. But in fact at any rate by the tenth century, and perhaps earlier, the command at this point in the service was understood to refer to the doors of the sanctuary, which were closed after the kiss of peace. A tenth-century text of the Liturgy directs the deacon to mount the ambo at the end of the anaphora and call for them to be opened again.

The same source, the Codex Pyromalus, shows that the creed was at·the time still sung by the whole congregation. The Codex Barberini too indicates that the people sang other parts of the service, including the Cherubic Hymn, the Sanctus and the

Lord's Prayer, and that they made the responses to the various greetings and exhortations.

The Anaphora

The creed finished, the anaphora began. Although the Codex Barberini could be taken to imply that the first part of the prayer was still recited audibly, it is practically certain that by the end of the eighth century the whole prayer was said silently, punctuated by certain phrases chanted out loud.

But if the people could not hear the greater part of the prayer, they could still see what was going on in the sanctuary. The description of the kiss of peace in the *De Ceremoniis* shows that there was no solid barrier between the sanctuary and the nave: the Emperor and the patriarch could exchange the kiss across the low chancel barrier. The custom of concealing the sanctuary during the anaphora by means of a curtain first appeared in the eleventh century in monastic circles. The chancel barrier was designed to provide a defined space for the clergy and to prevent access to the sanctuary by the laity: it was not intended to prevent the people seeing the altar and what went on at it. Whatever may have been the case elsewhere, in Constantinople the people could still participate visually in the offering of the gifts.

After the anaphora the bishop gave a blessing, as in the modern rite – no longer Chrysostom's 'Peace be with you all' – and there followed a litany accompanied by a prayer said silently by the bishop. The litany is only indicated in the Codex Barberini, but was no doubt not very different from that in the modern rite. The accompanying prayers are those of the present Liturgy. The Clementine Liturgy contained a litany at this point, concluded by a prayer said by the bishop, and it may be that the Byzantine rite also included it well before the end of the eighth century, even though the Codex Barberini is the first positive evidence for its existence.

The present form includes the 'angel of peace' biddings. The earliest form of this sequence is found in the fourth-century *Apostolic Constitutions*, where it occurs in the Eucharist after the prayers for the catechumens just before their dismissal. A similar sequence is found in the same source at the end of the final litany of morning and evening prayer. From their position it seems these petitions were considered suitable for those about to leave the church and resume their life in the world. They all, but especially the catechumens who have not yet been fortified by the grace of the Holy Spirit in baptism, need the support and guidance of their guardian angel in their struggle against the angel of darkness and evil spirits. They may have belonged originally to the dismissal of the catechumens: that is certainly the context in which Chrysostom mentions them. But they were obviously appropriate to the faithful too, and soon became part of their prayer at the end of the morning and evening services. They are to be found there in Vespers and Orthros in the Byzantine rite.

In the fully-developed Byzantine Liturgy they occur twice: in the litany after the Great Entrance, and in that before the Lord's Prayer after the anaphora, where alone the Codex Barberini mentions them. It is rather surprising it mentions them at all, since it does not normally indicate the presence of a litany at other points where we know one existed: it is a euchologion, not a complete text of the rite. Perhaps it indicates a recent introduction of these petitions into the litany at this point. The petitions for the acceptance of the gifts offered are certainly far older here.

It may be that the 'angel of peace' petitions found their way into this litany from the Liturgy of the Presanctified Gifts. That service consists essentially of Vespers followed by Communion from the reserved sacrament. The final litany of Vespers including these petitions is sung immediately before the Lord's Prayer, said in preparation for Communion. Perhaps by a process of assimilation they were added to the existing litany before that prayer in the Liturgy itself.

In the Liturgy of the Presanctified Gifts the same litany is preceded by the Great Entrance, in which the consecrated bread and a chalice of unconsecrated wine are brought in and set on the altar. It was perhaps this juxtaposition that led ultimately to the introduction of this litany after the Great Entrance in the present rites of St John Chrysostom and St Basil. It is not possible to say whether this happened before or after the introduction of the 'angel of peace' biddings into the litany after the anaphora. The fact that the Codex Barberini does not mention it is not decisive, given its lack of reference to most litanies. It is perhaps more likely that the petitions were first added to the existing litany after the anaphora some time before the ninth century, and that the litany after the Great Entrance was added later.

The Lord's Prayer was then said, followed by the greeting 'Peace be with you', and the deacon's command 'Let us bow our heads to the Lord'. The prayers supplied for the blessing traditionally given at this point are those of the present rite. The prayer in the second rite is to be said 'mystically', the doxology of both is to be said 'out loud'.

A prayer, in essence that of the present rite, was said by the priest in preparation for the elevation of the consecrated bread – another prayer of priestly devotion – and when the deacon had called the people to order by his cry 'Let us attend', the priest lifted up the consecrated bread above the paten, saying: 'Holy things for holy people'. This gesture had been mentioned by Maximus the Confessor, and seems to have been a natural development from the fifth-century gesture of the celebrant raising his hands at this point as an appeal for attention. The people made their traditional reply: 'One is holy, one is Lord, Jesus Christ, to the glory of God the Father.'

The Codex Barberini directs the priest to take portions from the consecrated bread and put them in the chalices. This presupposes a large number of communicants. As he does so he says, 'For the fullness of the Holy Spirit', a formula first found in an eighth-century translation into Armenian of the Liturgy of St John Chrysostom. There is no mention of the zeon in the Codex. It seems that it was not performed everywhere, and there are manuscripts of the Liturgy up to the fourteenth century which do not contain it.

We do not know precisely when and where the custom began of putting the bread into the chalice and giving communion with a spoon. The Council in Trullo of 692 forbade the use of any kind of receptacle for receiving Communion, and affirmed that the hands of a living man, made in the image and likeness of God, are the only appropriate receptacle for the sacrament of the Body of Christ. The spoon seems to have been introduced some time during the eighth century, and its use gradually spread. The practice was criticized by Western writers in the ninth century. After it had become general for the laity, the clergy continued to receive Communion in the traditional way.

During Communion a psalm was sung. The Codex Barberini provides a blessing immediately after Communion, 'O God save your people and bless your heritage', which is the sign for 'Let our mouths be filled with your praise' to be sung. A litany follows, probably much like the present one, while the priest says silently the prayer proper to each Liturgy, found in the present rite, though said there after the Communion of the clergy. A similar litany, followed by a prayer said out loud, is found in the

Clementine Liturgy; and some such form had no doubt been part of the Byzantine rite for some time.

When it was finished the deacon dismissed the people with 'Let us go forth in peace', and they replied 'In the name of the Lord'. The clergy processed out to the skeuophylakion as they had always done. Just beyond the ambo the bishop stopped to give the final blessing by saying the prayer behind the ambo. For the Liturgy of St Basil the Codex Barberini gives a prayer virtually identical with that now used in both Liturgies. A different prayer is given for the second rite. The present prayer was originally used on ordinary days. For festivals special 'prayers behind the ambo' were provided. Some forty different such prayers have survived: they fell into disuse in favour of a single fixed prayer only in the fourteenth century.

Back in the skeuophylakion there was, from the eighth century, a final prayer to be said, one for each rite.

Between the early seventh and early ninth centuries several important developments took place in the Liturgy at Constantinople, which make the period a turning-point in the history of Byzantine eucharistic worship. The prothesis appeared as the ritualized preparation of the elements before the beginning of the public service. To the beginning of that service were added the antiphons; and the synapte, or litany, was introduced after the entry and before the Trisagion. The ektene, or litany of fervent supplication, was inserted after the Gospel. These served to obscure the basic structure of the rite which had hitherto survived unencumbered.

Some of the most important prayers of the service, notably the anaphora, had already come to be recited inaudibly. This marked the beginning of the process whereby the people were gradually excluded from direct participation in the central action of the Eucharist. It began, too, the process whereby the Liturgy came to be divided into two: one part – the original core of the service – celebrated by the clergy in the sanctuary, inaudibly and later on invisibly; the other, led by the deacon, conducted simultaneously in the nave.

The growing clericalization of the service gave rise to an increasing number of prayers of devotion for the clergy, so encumbering still further the structure of the rite with secondary texts.

At the same time the tradition of interpreting the different moments of the rite symbolically provided the worshipper with a wealth of meanings he could attach to a service in whose central action he took less and less part.

The *Ecclesiastical History* of Germanos of Constantinople

One of the most widely used commentaries on the Liturgy was the *Ecclesiastical History*. In its original form it is now generally held to have been written by Germanos I, Patriarch of Constantinople from 715 to 730. A Latin version was sent to Charles the Bald by the Roman Anastasius the Librarian, who spent some time in Constantinople 869–70. The text he translated had already been added to, and in the following centuries still more additions and alterations were made to the *History*, in order to keep pace with developments in the Liturgy itself. It was sometimes copied with the text of the Liturgy, and in the sixteenth century a version of the work was printed alongside the first printed text of the three Liturgies: St John Chrysostom, St Basil, and the Liturgy of the Presanctified. It was regarded for many centuries as almost the official explanation of the rite.

The full title of Germanos' commentary is significant: *The Ecclesiastical History and Mystical Contemplation*. The latter part links the work with the approach of Maximus the Confessor and Dionysius the Areopagite, both of whom were concerned primarily with the contemplation of the eternal realities of which the Liturgy and its component parts were the symbols. Writing within the Alexandrian theological tradition they gave less prominence to the saving events in the life of Jesus Christ. Germanos is not without concern for this aspect of the meaning of the Liturgy. But he gives greater prominence to the contemplation of the events of salvation history – the 'historia', which also means contemplation, of the way in which God made himself known in the life, death and resurrection of Jesus, and which enables the worshipper to participate in the salvation which those events brought about. With the Alexandrian approach, already well established in the Byzantine tradition, Germanos united the concern with historical events and with the full humanity of Jesus of the Antiochene tradition.

Both aspects are apparent in his interpretation of the church building. 'The church is an earthly heaven in which the super-celestial God dwells and walks about'. But it also 'represents the crucifixion, burial and resurrection of Christ'. The apse represents both the cave of the nativity and the sepulchre. The holy table symbolizes both the place where the body of Christ was laid: it is also the throne of God, and the table of the Last Supper. The ciborium over the altar is there 'to represent concisely the crucifixion, burial and resurrection of Christ'. But if the altar represents the tomb of Christ, it also 'is and is called the heavenly and spiritual altar, where the earthly and material priests who always assist and serve the Lord represent the spiritual, serving and hierarchical powers of the immaterial and celestial Power'. The fulfilment of salvation history is symbolized too: for the bema – the sanctuary – and in particular the bishop's throne with the benches of the clergy point to the second coming of Christ to sit on his throne of judgement. Outside the sanctuary, the ambo in the middle of the nave stands for the stone rolled away from the entrance to the sepulchre, and so proclaims the resurrection.

Posture too has its meaning. Prayer is made towards the east because 'the comprehensible sun of righteousness, Christ our God, appeared on earth in those regions of the east where the perceptible sun rises'. The prohibition of kneeling on Sundays and throughout Eastertide is a sign 'that our fall has been corrected through the resurrection of Christ on the third day'.

Interpreting vesture, Germanos again combines Alexandrian and Antiochene approaches. The stole worn by the priests 'indicates the stole of the flesh of Christ dyed by his undefiled blood on the cross'. The unbelted phelonia of the priests show that 'even Christ thus went to the crucifixion carrying his cross'. At the same time 'the presbyters resemble the seraphic powers, covered, as if by wings, with stoles'. The oraria of the deacons, too, are the wings of the angelic powers of whom their wearers are the images. But the embroidery on the arms and sides of their robes represents the bonds with which Christ was bound, and the blood which flowed from his side. Germanos quotes from Isidore of Pelusium when he comes to the bishop's omophorion, which represents the lost sheep brought home on the Lord's shoulder.

When Germanos comes to explain the Liturgy itself it is the historical approach which predominates, though the earlier tradition of interpretation is not excluded. Nor does Germanos attempt to attach symbolic significance to the whole Liturgy. Once he reaches the anaphora, he speaks of the content and meaning of the prayer, and of the participation of the Church on earth in the worship of the Church in heaven.

Of the bread of offering Germanos says that 'it signifies the superabundant riches of the goodness of our God, because the Son of God became man and gave himself as an offering and oblation in ransom and atonement for the life and salvation of the world'. The prosphora stands for the bread which came down from heaven; and the piece cut out by the spear symbolizes the passion and death of Christ, which are also represented by the chalice, symbol of the blood and water which flowed from his pierced side. At the same time the bread and chalice are the memorial of the Last Supper. We have already seen how by the ninth century this interpretation had given rise, in the expanded version used by Anastasius, to the earliest rite of the prothesis, in which the actions are intended to be symbolic from the beginning, and set forth the passion and death of the Lord.

The representation of the history of salvation begins with the antiphons, which stand for the prophecies foretelling the coming of the Son of God in the incarnation. That coming itself is signified by the entrance of the Gospel: and the Good Shepherd who took the lost sheep of human nature upon himself – symbolized by the bishop's stole – is worshipped by the angelic host, whose 'Glory to God in the highest' is represented by the verse of the entry psalm, 94 (95).6, 'Come, let us worship and fall down before him'. The Trisagion too, sung to the Trinity, is the likeness of the angelic song at the birth of Christ.

Germanos is not entirely logical in his interpretation. For immediately after the incarnation, 'the ascent of the bishop to the throne and his blessing the people signifies that the Son of God, having completed the economy of salvation, raised his hands and blessed his holy disciples, saying to them: "Peace I leave with you" '. When the bishop sits, he represents the exaltation of the human nature assumed by God the Son, and the Father's acceptance of Christ's self-offering.

With the prokeimenon we are back to the prophecies of Christ's coming, while the censer, presumably used during the 'Alleluia' psalm, 'demonstrates the humanity of Christ, and the fire, his divinity. The sweetsmelling smoke reveals the fragrance of the Holy Spirit which precedes.' Anastasius had a more fanciful account in which the censer represents the sanctified womb of the Virgin, and the coal Christ.

The Gospel is again the coming of God in the incarnation. The bishop's blessing after it indicates the second coming of Christ, which the position of the bishop's fingers shows will be in 6,500 years.

125

When Germanos comments on the Great Entrance, it is partly in terms of the passion of Christ, following Theodore of Mopsuestia, though applying passion symbolism in greater detail. So he sees in the eileton, or corporal, a symbol of the winding-sheet prepared for the body of Christ; in the paten, or discos, the hands of Joseph and Nicodemus who buried him; and in the discos cover the cloth which covered his face in the tomb. The large veil, or aer, which was put over all the vessels on the altar, signifies the stone rolled over the entrance to the sepulchre. The place of Calvary is symbolized by the final preparation of the gifts in the skeuophylakion. Germanos here refers to the tradition that Christ was crucified on the spot where Adam was buried, and draws on patristic typology in pointing to the sacrifice of Abraham as a figure of the sacrifice of Christ.

This passion symbolism is combined with an explanation of the Great Entrance in the terms of the Cherubic Hymn, which, as we have seen, is to be understood as referring not simply to the Entrance itself, but to the whole celebration of the mysteries to which it leads. Of the procession and hymn Germanos says this:

> By means of the procession of the deacons and the representation of the fans, which are in the likeness of the seraphim, the Cherubic Hymn signifies the entrance of all the saints and righteous ahead of the cherubic powers and the angelic hosts, who run invisibly in advance of the great king, Christ, who is proceeding to the mystical sacrifice, borne aloft by material hands. Together with them comes the Holy Spirit in the unbloody and reasonable sacrifice. The Spirit is seen spiritually in the fire, incense, smoke, and fragrant air: for the fire points to his divinity, and the fragrant smoke to his coming invisibly and filling us with good fragrance through the mystical, living, and unbloody service and sacrifice of burnt-offering. In addition, the spiritual powers and choirs of angels, who have seen his dispensation fulfilled through the cross and death of Christ, the victory over death which has taken place, the descent into hell and the resurrection on the third day, with us exclaim the Alleluia.

> It is also in imitation of the burial of Christ, when Joseph took down the body from the cross, wrapped it in clean linen, anointed it with spices and ointment, carried it with Nicodemus, and placed it in a new tomb hewn out of a rock. The altar is an image of the holy tomb, and the divine table is the

sepulchre in which, of course, the undefiled and all-holy body was placed.

Once the gifts are placed on the altar and covered with the aer, Germanos' application of historical symbolism is almost at an end. The rest of the Liturgy is understood as the image of the worship of heaven, into which the worshipper on earth is introduced. The transition is made in this passage:

> Thus Christ is crucified, life is buried, the tomb is secured, the stone is sealed. In the company of the angelic powers, the priest approaches, standing no longer as on earth, but attending at the heavenly altar, before the altar of the throne of God, and he contemplates the great, ineffable, and unsearchable mystery of God.

Only the resurrection remains to be proclaimed, and that is done by the dialogue which introduces the anaphora, and the removal of the aer. The priest then leads everyone to the heavenly Jerusalem by his exhortation 'Let us lift up our hearts', and himself 'goes with confidence to the throne of the grace of God and, with a true heart and in certainty of faith, speaks with God'. 'Contemplating the heavenly liturgy', he 'is initiated even into the splendour of the life-giving Trinity'. The fans and the deacons are images of the seraphim and cherubim, 'for in this way earthly things imitate the heavenly, transcendent, the spiritual order of things'.

The remainder of the commentary consists of a description and explanation of the content of the anaphora, and of the Lord's Prayer. There is no further need for symbolism, for the celebration of the mysteries themselves is the realization of the redemption Christians have already received by grace. At the end of his account of the anaphora, and leading into his explanation of the Lord's Prayer, Germanos writes:

> Thereby having come into the unity of faith and communion of the Spirit through the dispensation of the one who died for us and is sitting at the right hand of the Father, we are no longer on earth but standing by the royal throne of God in heaven, where Christ is, just as he himself says: 'Righteous Father, sanctify in your name those whom you gave me, so that where I am, they may be with me' (cf. John 17). Therefore, receiving adoption and becoming co-heirs with Christ through his grace, and not through works, we have the spirit of the Son of God.

Contemplating his power and grace, the priest calls out, saying 'Abba, heavenly Father, make us worthy to say boldly and without condemnation'. . . .

The *Ecclesiastical History* of Germanos brings into the Byzantine tradition of liturgical interpretation, hitherto largely Alexandrian in its inspiration, the historical approach of the Antiochene school. It does so as part of the reaction against iconoclasm. Defenders of the icons based their argument on the orthodox doctrine of the incarnation: if God truly became fully human in Jesus Christ, then the incarnate Christ can be depicted pictorially. If part of the background to iconoclasm was the excessive insistence on the part of the monophysites on the divinity of Christ, to the detriment of his complete humanity, part of the orthodox reaction was to emphasize the historical, bodily nature of the incarnate Son. Germanos was one of the earliest defenders of icons and one of the first victims of the iconoclasts: he was deposed by the iconoclast Emperor Leo III. It is not surprising then that his exposition of the Liturgy should not only treat it in the traditional manner as an image of heavenly realities, but should draw upon the Antiochene tradition of Theodore of Mopsuestia in order to expound at least the first part of the rite as a representation of the earthly life of Christ.

It is important to notice that Germanos' commentary is not completely dominated by either or both of these approaches. He also expounds the essential significance of the Liturgy as a sacramental celebration in which the memorial of Christ's self-giving is made, and the reality of the future Kingdom, already inaugurated, is anticipated. Future commentators would not be so disciplined in their use of Antiochene historical symbolism. Yet Germanos anticipated their approach by the way he applied the principle of symbolic interpretation to details of the church and the service, so introducing a new dimension into the tradition of liturgical exposition. The *Ecclesiastical History* can be considered the first fully Byzantine commentary on the Liturgy.

7 The Byzantine Liturgy in the Eleventh Century

The Liturgy that has been described so far has been that of the Great Church in Constantinople, which as the rite of the capital can appropriately be called Byzantine, from the old name of the city. But it would be more proper now to speak of the Orthodox Liturgy. For by the eleventh century the Church of the Eastern Empire was not only distinct from that of the West, but was increasingly becoming separated from it by political, cultural and doctrinal differences which were sometimes brought into sharp focus by liturgical differences. At the same time the Byzantine Church was, on the one hand, becoming a Church increasingly ruled by tradition, and on the other, expanding into new territories largely outside the bounds of the shrinking Empire. The worship of the Church was becoming more and more uniform, with the rites of the Great Church displacing all other local rites within the Empire, and spreading to the new Churches founded among the Slav peoples.

Local differences still remained. But in the eleventh century Nicholas, Bishop of Andida in Pamphylia, was at pains to point out that the usages of his church conformed to those of the Great Church. Even in the ancient patriarchates, Alexandria, Antioch and Jerusalem, their traditional Liturgies were being influenced by that of Constantinople, whose prestige had steadily grown since the Muslim conquests of the seventh century, and the consequent decline of those Churches. By the end of the twelfth century the Byzantine canon lawyer and titular Patriarch of Antioch Theodore Balsamon gave it as his opinion that only the rite of Constantinople should be used by those who considered themselves Orthodox. The Byzantine Liturgy had become, to all intents and purposes, the Orthodox Liturgy.

It had certainly been received as such by the Slav Churches. Indeed it was the impression produced by the Liturgy in the Great Church on the emissaries of Vladimir, Prince of Kiev, which persuaded him to accept Christianity in its Byzantine form. The Russian *Primary Chronicle* relates how Vladimir sent some of his people to investigate the various religions of the world. They were not attracted to the Muslims in Bulgaria, nor impressed by the Latin worship of the Germans or Romans. But when they were taken to the Liturgy in the Great Church 'We knew not whether we were in heaven or on earth, for surely there is no such splendour or beauty anywhere upon earth. We cannot describe it to you: only this we know, that God dwells there among men, and that their service surpasses the worship of all other places. For we cannot forget that beauty.' For them Germanos' words were true: 'The church is an earthly heaven in which the supercelestial God dwells and walks about.' Vladimir was baptized in 988.

By the time of the conversion of the Slavs the Liturgy of the Great Church was well on its way to attaining its final form. But some developments were still to take place; and the eleventh century saw a number of them, constituting the penultimate stage of its growth. At the same time the decoration of the churches in which it was celebrated was being elaborated, providing the rite with a setting which closely corresponded with the developing tradition of liturgical interpretation.

The Church and its Decoration

By the eleventh century the characteristic church, found wherever Christianity had been spread from Constantinople, was of the cross-in-square kind. The central cupola over the nave might be flanked by smaller, lateral cupolas, and the sanctuary apse was accompanied at the east end by smaller apses to north and south. But by this time the restrained iconographic decoration of the ninth century had been somewhat elaborated. Three eleventh-century churches have survived with enough of their mosaic decoration to enable a good impression of the expanded scheme of this period to be formed. The monastery church of Hosios Lukas and the church of Daphne in Greece, and the church of the New Monastery on Chios, all represent a basically similar pattern of iconography.

The typical eleventh-century church was divided into three iconographic zones. The upper zone, consisting of the cupolas, high vaults, and semi-dome of the apse, represented heaven. It contained the images of Christ, the Virgin, and angels. The main cupola might contain one of three representations: the Christ Pantocrator, the ascension, or Pentecost. From the central medal-

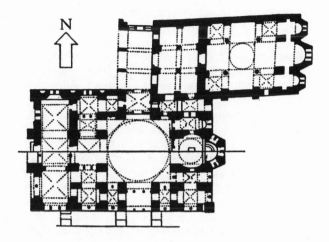

Plan of the catholicon of the monastery of Hosios Lukas, c. 1020, with the church of the Theotokos, c. 1040, in Greece.

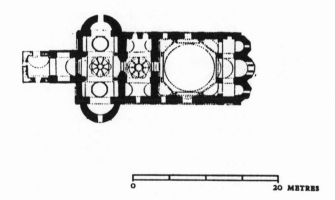

0   20 METRES

Plan of the catholicon, the principal church, of the New Monastery at Chios, 1042–1056.

131

lion containing the image angels, apostles or prophets radiated like the spokes of a wheel, facing each other across the space enclosed by the dome. The Christ Pantocrator became the predominant image in the central dome, superseding the older, more narrative image of the ascension. The representation of Pentecost might appear in another dome, or where there was only a single dome, in the vault above the sanctuary. The Christ Pantocrator also appeared in the narthex, above the main entrance into the church, together with the image of the Virgin and the representation of Christ as Immanuel.

The semi-dome of the apse was the place of the Mother of God, shown either standing or sitting enthroned. She was represented alone, against a gold background. Adoring angels were placed on the upper walls of the sanctuary, or on the vault above. Sometimes Christ was represented in the apse, as he had often been before the iconoclastic controversy. His image survived there in the later period in churches without domes, in which the apse was the highest symbolic space. Side apses, normal in the post-iconoclast period, generally contained images of John the Baptist, or of Joachim and Anna, representing the preparation for Christ's coming.

The second zone consisted of the upper parts of the vaults and the squinches or pendentives immediately below the cupolas. Here was represented the cycles of the great festivals, increasing in number as time went on. The full cycle included, by the eleventh century, the twelve feasts of the Annunciation, the Nativity, the Presentation of Christ in the Temple, the Baptism, the Transfiguration, the Raising of Lazarus, the Entry into Jerusalem, the Crucifixion, the Resurrection, or Harrowing of Hell, the Ascension, Pentecost, and the Falling Asleep of the Virgin. These were not at this time understood so much as historical scenes from the life of Jesus as images of the liturgical festivals. In the tenth and eleventh centuries they were not all necessarily represented in any particular church.

Such representations made present the different facets of the one mystery of Christ, his incarnation, passion and resurrection. Their presence did indeed make the church a representation of the crucifixion, burial and resurrection of Christ, as Germanos had stated it to be. The church itself was an active commemoration of the mighty works of God which were commemorated in the anaphora, and understood to be symbolized by the different parts of the Liturgy. The effectiveness of the scenes was

enhanced by placing them where possible in the curved pendentives of the central cupola. By this means Mary and Gabriel
actually faced each other across real space, the new-born Christ
was flanked by angels and other figures in the scene, and John the
Baptist and the angels really stand on either side of Jesus in the
Jordan. Not all the festival icons could be fitted into such ideal
spaces: some had to be placed on flat surfaces. Where the
pendentives of the cupola were small, they were often occupied
by images of the four evangelists instead.

The third and lowest zone was reserved for individual saints,
arranged in hierarchical order. In or near the sanctuary came the
patriarchs of the Old Testament and the hierarchs and teachers of
the Church. In the central part of the nave were the various
groups of martyrs; and in the western part of the nave the holy
monks. Holy women and canonized emperors were often in the
narthex. The saints were usually depicted standing, in such a way
as to emphasize that they and the worshippers belonged to the
same community. But they could also be shown as half figures, or
busts, placed in the smaller spaces of the building such as lunettes
or low shallow niches. Busts normally appeared in medallions on
arches, spandrels and narrow strips of wall. The selection of
saints represented depended to some extent on local preference.

These iconographic developments linked the eleventh-century
church still more closely than its ninth-century predecessor to the
Liturgy celebrated in it. Still heaven on earth and the communion
of saints, it was now also the representation of the saving work of
God in Christ by which earth was reunited with heaven, the
material universe transfigured, and mankind restored to the
paradise from which by sin it had fallen. Its correspondence with
the Liturgy which made present, in its whole and in its parts, the
saving mystery of Christ, could not fail to be clear to the
worshipper.

'The Concealment of the Mysteries'

We have seen that at Constantinople at any rate until the eleventh
century the congregation in the nave could see into the sanctuary.
Contrary to a widespread assumption, the sanctuary in Constantinople was not screened from view by curtains, nor was the
altar hidden by curtains drawn between the pillars of the ciborium. Representations of Byzantine sanctuaries and altars up to
the eleventh century in frescoes and miniatures show them open

to view. Some churches had in any case only a low chancel barrier without taller columns between which curtains could have been hung. In churches which had such columns, carrying an architrave, any images which might be associated with the chancel barriers were placed on top of the architrave, not between the columns. All the earlier Byzantine commentators on the Liturgy presuppose that the people can see what they describe and explain.

It is true that in other parts of the Church the sanctuary had long been concealed from the people during the anaphora. But the first clear reference to this custom so far as Constantinople is concerned appears in the *Protheoria*, a mid-eleventh-century interpretation of the Liturgy, which speaks of the closing of the doors of the chancel screen and the drawing of a curtain after the Great Entrance. The writer speaks of this as a monastic custom, and it was probably in monastic churches that it began in the latter part of the eleventh century.

Behind it lay the view that the laity ought not to see the accomplishment of the mysteries. Nicetas Stethatos, a monk of the monastery of Stoudios in the capital, wrote towards the end of the century:

> Know that the place of the laity in the assembly of the faithful during the anaphora is far from the divine altar. The interior of the sanctuary is reserved to the priests, deacons and subdeacons; the area outside near the sanctuary to the monks and other ranks of our hierarchy; behind them and the platform, to the laity ... How then from such a distance can the laymen, to whom it is not allowed, contemplate the mysteries of God accomplished with trembling by his priests?

The 'unsanctified glance' of the laity might not fall on the sacred mysteries; 'for the contemplation and vision of these mysteries are consecrated by God and the apostles only to the priests who offer' (*Letter* 8 of Nicetas Stethatos).

Distance alone in the Great Church and other large churches ensured that the people could not see what was being done in the sanctuary. But in smaller churches a curtain ensured that they should not overstep the bounds of a liturgical piety which now still further deprived the laity of any active part in the celebration of the Liturgy. For two centuries or more the most important prayers of the service had been inaudible to the people: soon the actions of the clergy were to be invisible as well.

Developments in the Rite

Few major developments affecting the order of the service remain
to be recorded after the ninth century. But developments were
taking place in the eleventh century, which if they had not yet
reached the capital, were later to influence the Liturgy of the
Great Church. They concerned chiefly the prothesis and the so-
called enarxis, the preliminary service of antiphons.

The Prothesis

The ceremonial of the preliminary preparation of the bread and
wine had changed little since the ninth century. A description of
the prothesis was written by an unknown eleventh-century
patriarch of Constantinople for the benefit of Bishop Paul of
Gallipoli; it differs little from the ninth-century version of
Germanos' commentary translated by Anastasius the Librarian.
The only difference of note is that by the eleventh century only a
portion of the prosphora is offered: the deacon or priest cuts out a
piece from the prosphora with the spear and puts it on the paten.
In the Great Church this was still done by the deacon: elsewhere
priests were taking over the deacon's traditional function of
preparing the gifts.

The patriarch's account made no mention of incense. The
interpolated version of the *Ecclesiastical History* refers to incense,
and so do other sources, of the tenth and eleventh centuries. An
Arab version of the Liturgy of St John Chrysostom, perhaps of
the tenth century, provides for the paten veil to be put on while
the priest says: 'The Lord is king and has put on glorious
apparel.' He puts on the veil over the chalice, saying: 'The Lord
has put on his apparel and girded himself with strength.' Then he
covers both with the large veil and says: 'He has made the round
world so sure that it cannot be moved: his might has covered the
heavens with a veil and the earth is filled with his praise.' He
finishes the psalm and censes the gifts three times.

The prothesis began, and continued, as a preliminary rite in
which the people took no part. But one development which began
towards the end of the eleventh century linked it with popular
piety in a way which has continued to the present. Towards
the end of the century several prosphorae came to be used,
quite apart from their necessity when there were large numbers of communicants. Nicholas Grammaticus, Patriarch of

Constantinople 1084–1111 prescribed the use of four, one representing the Lord, another the Mother of God, a third the archangels and all the angelic orders, and a fourth the Forerunner, John the Baptist, the apostles, prophets. holy bishops, and all the saints. Further prosphorae might be offered for the living and the departed. From all these particles were cut out and placed on the paten.

The laity brought prosphorae to church in commemoration of those for whom they wished prayer to be offered. Some have thought this to be a new custom in the eleventh century; more probably it was the continuation of the early Christian custom whereby the people brought the bread and wine for the Eucharist to church. But whether new or old, the custom became an integral part of popular eucharistic devotion, and one of the few ways in which they could participate actively in the celebration of the Liturgy. The typikon drawn up by the Empress Irene for a monastery she had founded well illustrates the importance of these commemorations for laypeople:

> Concerning how many loaves are to be offered at each Liturgy and on whose behalf: each day at the holy Liturgy seven loaves are to be offered, one the Lord's, another for our Lady full of grace and the Mother of God, another for the saint of the day, another for the remission and forgiveness of sins of my most mighty Emperor (her husband Alexios Comnenos) and myself, another for the monks who have died, another for our departed parents and other relations, and another for our children who are alive and for our families and relatives.

The commemorations were made by means of particles taken from each prosphora, and the names were inscribed in the diptychs of the living and the departed.

The Enarxis

The Liturgy in Constantinople still began with the antiphons, and the Great Litany was sung after the entry of the Gospel, or Little Entrance, and before the Trisagion. Elsewhere, however, it was sung before the antiphons, in its present place. Sometimes it was sung there only, sometimes it continued to be sung, perhaps somewhat shortened, before the Trisagion as well. Only from the thirteenth century was it used exclusively in its present position, so fixing the old prayer of the faithful at the beginning of the

Liturgy of the Catechumens, as the first part of the rite came to be called.

By the eleventh century the antiphons were sung in their present form. But outside Constantinople the Typika were sometimes sung as an alternative introduction. They entered in time the rite of the Great Church and in some churches entirely supplanted the antiphons. They consist of Psalms 103, 146 followed by the troparion 'Only-begotten Son', and the Beatitudes. Followed outside the Liturgy by the creed, a prayer of absolution, the Lord's Prayer, a variable contakion, the forty-fold Kyrie eleison, Psalm 33 and a dismissal they constitute a separate office, found in the Horologion after Sext or None.

The office of the Typika, or typical psalms, in its full form was the Palestinian monastic equivalent of the Liturgy of the Presanctified. First found in the ninth century, it was a form for receiving Communion from the reserved sacrament on days when the Liturgy was not celebrated. When the monasteries of Constantinople adopted the daily office used in Palestine, as prescribed in the Typikon of St Sabas, they adopted with it the use of the Typika. In the famous monastery of Stoudios in the capital it was sung after the Liturgy on days when work did not permit the celebration of the lesser hours. It was no longer used as a communion office: instead the antidoron was distributed at its conclusion. When the lesser hours were sung, the Typika were sung after None.

In the twelfth century the monks of the Evergetis monastery in the capital regularly used the two psalms and the Beatitudes from the Typika instead of the older antiphons. During the distribution of the antidoron after the prayer behind the ambo they sang Psalm 33 (34), the former communion psalm of the Typika. They still used the entry verse of the old third antiphon, Psalm 95, 'O come let us worship and fall down before Christ'. When the office of the Typika first appeared, in the ninth century, the Beatitudes had their own refrain, 'Remember us, Lord, when you come into your kingdom' (Luke 23.42). At the Evergetis monastery special troparia were used instead. The Typika were used on most days when the full Liturgy was celebrated.

In the fourteenth century the *Diataxis* of Philotheos, an Athonite monk who later became Patriarch of Constantinople, prescribed the Typika for every celebration of the Liturgy. This was presumably the custom prevailing at the time on the Holy Mountain. In other places the antiphons were still used. Psalm 33

(34), 'I will always give thanks to the Lord', became a normal part of the Liturgy, preceded by the verse 'Blessed be the name of the Lord henceforth and for ever' (Psalm 113.2), which was part of the office of the Typika in the Horologion, though not part of the ninth-century communion office. The function of the prayer behind the ambo as the final prayer of the Liturgy was thus obscured.

The secondary character of both the prothesis and the enarxis continued to be shown by the fact that they were presided over by a priest even at a Liturgy celebrated by a bishop.

The Conclusion of the Rite

In the eleventh century the prayer behind the ambo was still the concluding prayer of the Liturgy. What Nicholas of Andida says about it is of great interest, since he shows that the laity were by no means all reconciled to the practice of inaudible recitation of the major prayers of the service.

> The prayer behind the ambo is the seal of all prayers and their recapitulation, worthy of the first and most honoured of epilogues. For the holy Liturgy is celebrated principally for those who have offered and for those on whose behalf they have offered: but also for the rest this one prayer makes it up. For some of those who stand outside the sanctuary are often thrown into doubt and confusion, saying: 'What is the point, and what is the sense or force of the prayers whispered by the bishop?'. And they want to know what these are, too. Therefore the holy fathers devised the form of this prayer as the recapitulation of everything that is asked for in the prayers, teaching those who wanted to know the cloth from the hem of the garment.

After the prayer behind the ambo the antidoron is distributed. It consisted of the remains of the prosphorae from which the portion representing Christ and the commemorative particles had been cut out. It was blessed, but not consecrated. As its name suggests, it was distributed as a substitute for Communion, which by this time few laypeople received frequently. Its precise origin is not clear: it served as a way of disposing of the prosphorae, and as break-fast for those who had fasted before Communion. As a substitute for Communion it gradually attracted to itself devotional practices properly linked with receiving the sacrament itself: in some churches it was received fasting, and at least in Romanian came to be called itself *anafora*.

The *Protheoria* of Nicholas of Andida

If little else had changed in the Liturgy since the ninth century, its interpretation underwent a development in the mid-eleventh-century *Protheoria*. Written by Nicholas, Bishop of Andida in Pamphylia, between 1054 and 1067, it was apparently rewritten by his successor Theodore, who tidied up his predecessor's work without making any significant changes in it.

But the *Protheoria* itself does make a significant change in the way the Liturgy is presented for the worshipper's contemplation. It was written by a bishop for his clergy, who were no doubt meant to pass on its understanding to their congregations. In this it differs from the *Ecclesiastical History*, written for laypeople, and Maximus' *Mystagogia*, written for monks. Both of these commentaries continued to be copied and read, so that a variety of approaches to participation in the Liturgy coexisted at the same time. Nicholas seems to have been dissatisfied with the approach of Germanos. He refers his readers to the *History* for an interpretation of the church and of the clergy's vestments. But he considers it unsatisfactory to confine the symbolism of the Liturgy to the passion, death and resurrection of Christ, as Germanos had on the whole done. For Nicholas the Liturgy is also a representation of the birth and early life of Christ, as he makes clear at the beginning of the *Protheoria*:

> Many who exercise the office of a priest know and confess that those things which are accomplished in the holy Liturgy are a type of the Saviour's passion, and of the burial and resurrection of Christ our God. But I do not know why they are, as I think, unaware that they also represent the whole of his saving coming and economy for us from the beginning: his conception, birth and the thirty years of his life; also the work of his Forerunner, and his manifestation at his baptism; then the calling of the apostles, and the three years in which he performed miracles, which were the cause of envy and the cross. For that is not called a body which has a head but lacks feet and hands and other members. But that it was a perfect body which was offered in sacrifice listen to Christ himself saying 'Take, eat, this is my body'. The story of someone's life

139

and activity cannot be told unless from the beginning are related those things which accompanied his birth, those which happened during the course of his life, and those which belong to its end.

Defending his intention of showing how the Liturgy represents the whole life of Christ Nicholas refers to the icons, which also depict the various stages of his life from its beginning to its end:

But there is a third confirmation of what has been said above, which has been handed down to the holy churches of God in a good and pious way together with the sacred Liturgy. What is it? It is the erection of the holy images by means of colours. For in them are related for the pious to see all the mysteries of the incarnation of Christ, from the coming of the archangel Gabriel to the Virgin to the Lord's ascension into heaven and his second coming.

The comparison is apt: for Nicholas goes on to depict the Liturgy as a series of images, representing in order the life and work of Christ. But he makes it clear from the beginning that the symbolic significance of the Liturgy is not always simple. For if it is true that 'every believer ought to know that the whole rite of the holy Liturgy represents the whole economy of the saving condescension for our sake of our true God and saviour Jesus Christ . . . by means of the mysteries accomplished in it', it is also true that 'one of those things which are accomplished in the Liturgy is to be understood as referring to two or three of the things which took place then'.

Explaining the prothesis, Nicholas sees in the prosphora from which the portion to be consecrated is cut a symbol of Mary, from whom the Word took flesh. The deacon who cuts it out is a figure of Gabriel. The place of the prothesis represents Bethlehem, and also Nazareth and Capernaum. In sum it represents the thirty years of Christ's life before his baptism. While the prepared gifts wait in the prothesis, the priest who begins the enarxis symbolizes John the Baptist and his ministry, preparing the way for Christ. The antiphons he calls prophetic readings. The troparion 'Only-begotten Son' 'is eminently adapted to the symbols of Christ's birth: for he who is born is the only-begotten Son and Word of the eternal Father, who vouchsafed for our salvation to be incarnate of the holy Mother of God, his godhead remaining unchanged and unconfused'. His consubstantiality with the

Father and the Holy Spirit is indicated by the singing of the Trisagion, which, following Byzantine tradition, Nicholas understands to be sung to the Trinity.

The entry of the bishop into the sanctuary during the third antiphon 'indicates the appearance and manifestation of Christ our God at the Jordan'. Nicholas refers to the black marble stripes laid at regular intervals in the floor of the Great Church, which were apparently called rivers. The priest yielding the presidency of the service to the bishop at this point illustrates the words of the Baptist: 'He must increase and I must decrease'. The ascent of the bishop to his throne signifies the passage from the Law and the Old Covenant to the beginning of divine grace: the prokeimenon is so called because it comes before all the symbols of the new grace.' The reading of their Acts and Epistles points to the calling of the apostles.

Nicholas is sensitive to the possible criticism that the Acts and Epistles were written after the passion of Christ, whereas in his interpretation their reading is made to signify things that took place earlier. His defence reveals his understanding of liturgical symbolism:

> But he who says this should know that neither enigma, symbol nor parable is able to preserve an exact similarity with what it represents; neither can they preserve the likeness of, much less identify with, persons, times and sequences. But they represent these things as being the image of the prototype.

The symbol, in other words, need have no close relationship with what it symbolizes. This helps to explain why a good deal of Nicholas' interpretation seems artificial and forced. The Liturgy is made to fit into a preconceived pattern of interpretation which does not arise out of the rite itself.

The Gospel represents the words of Christ. It is preceded by the 'Alleluia', during which the church is censed. Commenting on the chant, Nicholas takes up the traditional theme of the unity of the Church's worship with that of the angels. But he quickly moves on to apply his basic principle of interpretation to the censing, which 'symbolizes the grace of the Holy Spirit given to the disciples when he sent them out to heal every sickness and every disease in Israel'. The prayers and supplications which follow the Gospel represent the three years' teaching ministry of Christ.

The Great Entrance procession represents the Lord's journey

141

from Bethany to Jerusalem on Palm Sunday. The real significance of the Cherubic Hymn is not lost in the midst of Nicholas'
interpretation: 'The Cherubic Hymn which is sung admonishes
everyone from now on and until the end of the Liturgy to pay
great attention with their mind and to put away worldly and
earthly care, as those who are about to receive the great king in
communion.' But then he continues with a passage which well
shows the somewhat fanciful lengths to which the tradition of
symbolic interpretation led in the *Protheoria*:

> The placing of the holy things on the holy table represents now
> the upper room made ready, and a little later the lifting up of
> the cross. Finally it represents the burial, the resurrection, and
> the ascension. In order not to define the hour and time and
> place of each one of the things which took place then, the
> blessed fathers, lest other transfers and more altars should be
> needed, and the mystery of the economy be made foolish
> because of them ... set up a roof over the holy table. The
> enclosed and circumscribed holy floor between the four col-
> umns of the ciborium they separated off as representing the
> whole earth. By this the prophetic word was fulfilled which
> said: 'who wrought salvation in the midst of the earth' (Psalm
> 74.12). For since all confess that Jerusalem is situated in the
> middle of the earth, in which city the Lord endured all his
> passion, betrayal, judgement, and those things which preceded
> and followed the cross: since the holy table is seen to occupy
> the space between heaven and earth, and is situated in the
> midst of the columns and of the fans which surround it, it is
> naturally said to be under heaven: and so whether in India or
> the British Isles it indicates that salvation has been wrought in
> the midst of the earth by those things that are accomplished on
> it. But for him who says, not every church has a ciborium with
> its base and columns, it is enough for the semicircle of the bema
> (the apse) to be constituted in every church: whose curve
> represents the hemisphere of heaven, having in its midst,
> opposite, the holy table.

When he speaks of the dialogue before the anaphora, Nicholas'
comments are revealing. He gives the deacon's initial exhortation
as: 'Let us stand aright, let us stand with fear, let us pay attention
to the holy anaphora.' The final clause in fact reads in the text of
the Liturgy: 'Let us attend, that we may offer in peace the holy
oblation.' The original in each case is 'anaphora'. But Nicholas
understands the word, not in its technical Christian sense of

sacrificial offering, but in its non-theological sense of reference to:

> What is the anaphora? It means looking to the prototypes of the mysteries being performed. The name 'anaphora' is indicative of this and resembles its meaning: and therefore trembling and weeping we stand soberly and constantly as though we now saw the God-man suffering for us, so that in peace and without the distraction of earthly thoughts offering and relating these things we may be made worthy to see his holy resurrection, and be filled with the joy which comes from it: and especially those who receive the Body as the holiness of the place requires, for these suffer with him and being buried with him rise again with him.

Nicholas recognizes the sacramental reality of Communion and urges those who can to receive it every day. But he assumes that the active offering of the Eucharist is done by the priests, not as the mouthpiece of the people, but as their own proper action. The people only pay attention: their participation is by seeing the drama of Christ's life enacted in the symbols of the Liturgy.

Even the details of that drama are represented. The closing of the sanctuary doors and the drawing of the curtain, with the placing of the aer over the gifts on the altar, signify the night on which Jesus was betrayed, and the night trial: the removal of the aer, the drawing back of the curtain and opening of the doors signify the morning on which he was led away and handed over to Pilate. Even the precise wording of the narrative of institution in the anaphora is significant: of the bread the Lord said: 'Take, eat', of the cup he said: 'Drink of this all of you'. That is because Judas did not eat the bread but kept it and showed it to the Jews: he could not conceal any of the wine. That was why the phrase, 'For I will not reveal the mystery to your enemies', was added to the chant 'At your mystical supper'. The fans, shaped like cherubim and waved by deacons throughout the anaphora, represent the heavenly powers present with the Lord, especially in his final agony.

The central events of the death and resurrection of Christ are attached to details. The elevation of the bread at 'Holy things for holy people' signifies the lifting up of Christ on the cross, his death and his resurrection. The removal of the gifts after Communion from the altar to the prothesis represents the ascension, and their final censing the gift of the Holy Spirit.

Nicholas wrote within the tradition to whose formation all the writers we have so far looked at contributed. From Dionysius he took his concept of the ministry and of its function of initiating the faithful into an understanding of the mysteries. From Maximus he inherited his understanding of the church building as sacred space. He referred to the *History*, which he set out not to duplicate but to supplement. In practice he did more than supplement; for unlike Germanos he concentrated almost entirely on interpreting the Liturgy in terms of the historical life of Christ. He makes passing reference to the Old Testament types of the Eucharist in the patristic tradition, and to the Liturgy as reflecting the worship of heaven. But he was concerned above all to present the Liturgy to his clergy, and through them to the people, as a series of images portraying the life of Christ for their visual contemplation. There is little or no organic connection between the symbol and the reality symbolized: the liturgical rite is arbitrarily fitting into a preconceived pattern of interpretation in an over-elaborate and highly artificial way.

Nicholas' treatise, rewritten by Theodore, enjoyed considerable influence. It was put into verse by Michael Psellos some time between 1063 and 1067, perhaps for the edification of his imperial pupil, the future Michael VII. Parts of it were incorporated into the explanation of the church and the Liturgy sometimes attributed to a Patriarch Sophronius of Jerusalem, which also drew on the *History*. The *Protheoria* continued to be copied up to the fifteenth century, in both Nicholas' and Theodore's versions.

8 The Completion of the Liturgy

By the fourteenth century the Orthodox Liturgy had reached the full term of its development, and a process of consolidation was under way. Local variations in practice continued to exist in the Orthodox world. But the widespread influence of the *Diataxis* of Philotheos helped to establish a basic uniformity in the celebration of the Liturgy in all the churches of the Byzantine commonwealth.

Philotheos was a monk of Mount Athos who became Patriarch of Constantinople in 1354. Two rival Typika, or sets of rules for celebrating the services of the Church, were in use in the city. The traditional Typikon of the Great Church was that which originated in the ninth century in the monastery of St John of Stoudios. But by the twelfth century the Typikon of the monastery of St Sabas near Jerusalem was gradually gaining ground, not least because it gave more detailed instructions for the celebration of the services.

While still on the Holy Mountain Philotheos drew up two *Diataxeis*, one regulating the priest's and deacon's part in Matins, Vespers and the Liturgy, and one giving detailed directions for the celebration of the Liturgy. It established the text of the rites as well as the ceremonial to be observed. Its widespread use brought a uniform order into the Liturgy, particularly in the performance of the prothesis, which had the largest number of variations. It was introduced into the Great Church when Philotheos became Patriarch, and quickly spread to the Slav as well as the Greek Churches. Its rubrics were incorporated into the first printed service books in the sixteenth century.

The Setting of the Liturgy

By the fourteenth century the cross-in-square planned church was still widely found, but now alongside other designs. The Greek cross shape returned, and basilican-style churches were built too. Each part of the Orthodox world evolved its own

145

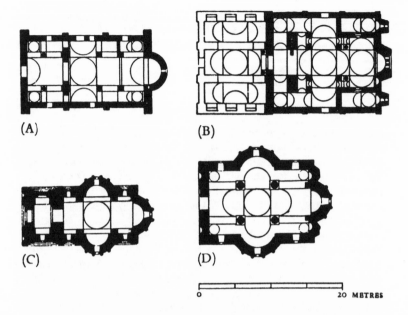

Ground plans of fourteenth-century churches (Yugoslavia). A. Staro Nagoricane, 1313; B. Gracanica, 1321; C. Krusevac, c. 1380; D. Ravanica, 1375–7.

characteristic variants on the basic themes, and a good many churches of the twelfth to fifteenth centuries have survived to enable us to study the setting in which the Liturgy was, and continues to be, celebrated. Many still have some or all of their decoration. The domed nave and the three apses at the east end continued to be normal.

In later Byzantine churches the sanctuary never projected into the nave. The chancel barrier ran below the arch separating the nave from the sanctuary apse, and usually continued north and south to screen the prothesis and the diakonicon. These usually communicated with the sanctuary within the screen through arches, as well as with the nave through doors. The prothesis was now an essential part of the building, and those churches which had formerly had separate skeuophylakia were provided with the two side rooms, often built onto the original church. By the fourteenth century the Great Church itself had been provided with an internal prothesis. The existence of three separate spaces

146

at least meant that the two entrances, with the Gospels and the prepared gifts, were processions from one place to another. In time the development of the iconostasis with three doors made it possible, in churches with only a single apse, for the prothesis to be a side table within the sanctuary itself, so that the processions began where they finished, and became purely ceremonial movements deprived of all practical significance.

The Development of the Iconostasis

It was only in the fourteenth century that the sanctuary came to be completely shut off from the sight of the congregation by a solid screen. The low chancel barrier, surmounted by columns carrying an architrave, which continued to be the means of distinguishing nave from sanctuary up to the thirteenth century, can still sometimes be seen behind the later fully-fledged screen.

Images had been associated with the chancel barrier from an early time. Representations of Christ, Mary, angels and saints had been carved on the architrave or placed on top of it. By the ninth century it had become customary to display certain icons for veneration near the chancel barrier: in front of it or behind it, on special stands; attached to its doors or columns, or to the upper part of the ciborium; or on top of the architrave. The latter arrangement can still be seen in the Byzantine-style cathedral of Torcello, near Venice, dating from the late eleventh or twelfth century. Two icons particularly associated with the sanctuary in one or other of these positions were the Christ Pantocrator and the Virgin shown in an attitude of supplication for mankind. Also popular was the deesis: Christ Pantocrator with the Virgin and John the Baptist in supplication on either side. With these or instead of them on the architrave might be apostles, saints and angels, or representations of some of the great festivals. Symeon of Thessalonike in his fifteenth-century commentary on the church and the Liturgy seems to presuppose the deesis with angels, apostles and saints represented on top of the architrave.

Most churches still had the typical Byzantine chancel barrier at the beginning of the fifteenth century. But it was in process of being transformed into what is now regarded as the typical Orthodox iconostasis. The icons of Christ and the Mother of God had only a short distance to move in order to occupy their now traditional places in the screen, to south and north respectively of the holy doors. The annunciation, often to be found in the

147

spandrels of the arch above the chancel barrier, came down to occupy the upper panels, or the whole, of the doors themselves. The deesis remained above the architrave, and so did the great festivals, expanded to form a complete series and placed above the deesis, to which further saints were added, all turned towards the central figure of Christ in supplication. As the iconostasis, or templon as it was often called, grew, further rows of prophets and patriarchs were placed above the festival icons. At its highest point of development the iconostasis completely filled the archway of the apse, totally cutting off the sanctuary from the nave. It is generally held that this form was developed in Russia and spread thence to Mount Athos, and on to the Greek and other Slav churches.

The effect of this development was to complete the process by which the people were cut off both from hearing the central prayers and seeing the central actions of the Liturgy. These became the exclusive preserve of the clergy, who alone by virtue of their ordination could hear, see and touch the mysteries which were too holy for the laity to approach, and which they only rarely received in communion. Popular eucharistic devotion was focused on the icons which they could venerate and before which they could pray, and on those parts of the service which they could hear or see. These too they might well be taught to regard as a series of icons, in which they could contemplate the saving life and work of Christ.

The Decoration of the Church

By the fourteenth century the middle Byzantine scheme of church decoration had developed considerably. It was perhaps inevitable that the somewhat austere scheme worked out in the period immediately after the victory of the icons should have undergone amplification. The expansion that took place was encouraged by developments both in architecture and in the medium of decoration. Middle Byzantine decoration was executed in mosaic, and confined to certain areas of the church. The lower walls were usually faced with marble. By the fourteenth century mosaic had almost entirely been replaced by the cheaper medium of fresco painting. Figured marble and mosaic gave way to plastered interiors entirely covered with painting. The restricted cycle of themes used in the tenth and eleventh centuries was extended to provide the subject-matter needed to fill the whole building. The revival of the basilican plan meant that there were long stretches of wall to be filled. The hierarchical, sacramental arrangement of middle Byzantine mosaics could not be reproduced successfully in such churches. Narrative sequences, such as had been used before iconoclasm, began to appear again.

Not only had church decoration greatly expanded, incorporating new themes: it had also been considerably influenced by the Liturgy and its interpretation, and by the calendar which regulated the Church's year. The basic themes of the earlier period remained, but they were now set in a rich variety of narrative sequences which took little notice of the division of the church into different spaces with distinct functions, but spread throughout the building.

The apse almost invariably contained the image of the Mother of God. It was understood to be linked with the Liturgy celebrated in the sanctuary below. Through Mary the Word became flesh and was manifest in the world: through the Liturgy Christ's incarnation and appearing were set forth for the Church to contemplate. Below was represented the communion of the apostles, of which the earliest example dates from the eleventh century in Kiev. There in Hagia Sophia Christ is depicted twice, on either side of an altar covered by a ciborium. On one side apostles come to receive the bread, on the other the cup. This is one of the new themes of iconography, which departs from the strict rules of iconodule theology, for it does not represent a historical scene: Christ gives Communion to the apostles in the way in which the bishop distributes the sacrament to the faithful. But the scene reflects admirably the teaching of the commentaries, in which the Liturgy celebrated on earth is both an image of the Last Supper, and a representation of the worship of heaven, and the bishop is the figure of Christ. The Communion of the apostles combines historical, liturgical and spiritual realities in one image.

Beneath the Communion of the apostles come representations of the liturgists, that is, of bishops in their liturgical vestments. St Basil and St John Chrysostom naturally occupy the chief place, often with St Gregory the Great, the traditional author of the Liturgy of the Presanctified. They might be escorted by deacons such as Stephen or Laurence. Sometimes they face the actual altar, sometimes one is depicted in the centre of the apse wall. Carrying liturgical texts, the holy bishops of the past are as it were heavenly concelebrants with those who stand at the earthly altar.

On the walls of the sanctuary, between the apse and the nave, there were often representations of the Old Testament types of the Eucharist, such as we have seen in the church of San Vitale in Ravenna: the sacrifice of Abel – referred to in the prayer of the proskomidia in the Liturgy of St Basil; Melchisedech bringing bread and wine; the sacrifice of Isaac by Abraham; and the hospitality of Abraham. The latter has a eucharistic as well as a trinitarian significance: the table around which the three angels are sitting is often shown as an altar, on which rests a chalice, or dish, containing a lamb. Participation in the Eucharist takes the worshipper into the heart of the Trinity, whose very nature is self-giving love.

Liturgical themes were particularly in evidence in the decoration of the prothesis. In the semi-dome of the apse St John the Baptist is often depicted, in accordance with Nicholas of Andida's interpretation of the rite of the prothesis as symbolizing the incarnation and its prophetic foretelling. Passion symbolism was prominent. Christ might be shown as a child on a paten, a bishop piercing his side with a spear, illustrating Germanos' interpretation of the proskomidia in the version of Anastasius. Sometimes Christ is shown dead and prepared for burial. But he might also be shown as a child, without the passion symbolism, and then Nicholas' birth symbolism is to the fore.

The Christ Pantocrator still looked down from the central dome, unless in a basilican church without a dome his image had been moved to the next holiest place, the semi-dome of the apse. But by now it had become usual to place round the lower edge of the dome, or round the drum supporting it, a representation of the heavenly Liturgy. Like the Communion of the apostles, out of which it may have developed, this scene broke away from strict iconodule theology. It takes the form of the Great Entrance procession, transposed into heavenly terms, in which angelic priests and deacons, carrying lights, fans and liturgical instruments, move towards an altar. That the Great Entrance could be used as a shorthand symbol for the whole Liturgy shows how prominent a part it had come to occupy both in the rite itself and in Byzantine liturgical piety. Sometimes the procession is shown leaving one altar, the prothesis, and moving to another. Sometimes Christ is shown, robed as a bishop, waiting for the procession to arrive at the altar. He might be depicted, in addition, standing at the prothesis, having sent the procession on its way.

The cycle of major festivals depicting the major events in the life of Christ continued to appear on the upper parts of the walls and vaults of the church. They were now supplemented by other scenes, not strictly festivals, such as Christ among the doctors and the unbelief of Thomas, which might be commemorated on a particular day. Just as the commemoration of the incarnate life of Christ had become more detailed in the symbolic interpretation of the Liturgy, so iconography included more and more scenes illustrating the same basic mystery.

By the fourteenth century other cycles had been added to the decoration of the church. They were of a narrative kind, and had no particular connection with the principal cycle of Christ's life. They might be found in different parts of the church. The life of the Virgin might be in its aisles and side-chambers, or in the narthex. The dormition however was usually on the west wall of the nave. This cycle corresponds in part with the commemoration of the Mother of God in the calendar, and with such semi-liturgical devotions to her as the Akathistos hymn.

Another secondary cycle often found in the aisles and narthex, as well as sometimes in the nave, represents the teaching and miracles of Christ. Cabasilas, in his commentary on the Liturgy, emphasizes that it is primarily the commemoration of the passion, death and resurrection of Christ, not of his miracles. The passion itself was sometimes represented in a detailed sequence of scenes, apart from the image of the crucifixion in the festival sequence.

To the representations of individual saints, which continued to adorn the lower parts of the nave walls in hierarchical order were now added cycles showing the life of a particular saint, perhaps the saint in whose honour the church was dedicated, or one or more of those held in high esteem in the locality, or in the Church at large.

From the thirteenth century it was customary to depict the seven ecumenical councils, in the narthex or side-chambers, or in the porch. By now they were all the object of celebrations included in the calendar, that of the seventh council being celebrated on the first Sunday of Lent as the Feast of Orthodoxy, the Church's victory over all the heresies. Their inclusion in the decoration of churches reflected the controversy with the Western Church over the precise number of councils to be reckoned

151

ecumenical, and their place near the entrance served to emphasize the church as the pillar and ground of right belief about the incarnation of Christ to which the whole building bore witness.

One further representation which appeared in the fourteenth century was the Last Judgement. This too is linked with the calendar, in which the second Sunday before Lent was the Sunday of the Last Judgement. In the Liturgy it links up with the commemoration of the dead in the proskomidia, and is a reminder of the prayers which ask that those who communicate may do so not for judgement or condemnation but for salvation of soul and body. The representation was sometimes in the narthex, sometimes in one of the side chapels used for the commemoration of the dead or for funerals. At Voroneţ in Romania it occupies the whole of the exterior of the west wall of one of the five famous painted churches.

The connection between the extended scheme of decoration of the fourteenth century and the calendar is explicit in the representation of the calendar often found in the narthex, in which scenes depicting the main feasts in each month are arranged in order round the walls.

The expanded iconography of the fourteenth century, while it included the elements of the classical middle Byzantine scheme, contained a good deal of narrative material less closely related to the original principles of iconic representation. In addition it embraced scenes in which historical and non-historical elements were confused, invisible realities being depicted in terms of their earthly images. Perhaps this was natural enough in a century in which Gregory Palamas defended the hesychast monks of Mount Athos, and affirmed that in the Liturgy it was possible to see Christ visibly with the eye of faith:

This house of God here is a true symbol of that tomb . . . For behind the curtain it has the room in which the body of Christ will be laid and there too the holy altar. Whoever therefore hastens to draw near to the divine mystery and the place where it is, and who perseveres to the end . . . will without doubt see the Lord with his spiritual, yes, I say, even with his physical eyes. Whoever sees the mystical meal with faith, and the bread of life which is offered there, sees under the outward forms the divine Word himself, who for us became flesh and dwells in us as in a temple.

The Liturgy in the Fourteenth Century

The *Diataxis* of Philotheos shows that the Liturgy in the mid-fourteenth century had, in all save a few details, acquired the form in which it is celebrated today. Such development as had occurred since the eleventh century had taken place in the proskomidia, and in the private devotions of the clergy. By now the Liturgy of St John Chrysostom had become the normal rite, by a process which seems to have begun in the twelfth century. The rite of St Basil came eventually to be used on only ten occasions in the year. From the worshipper's point of view it made little difference, since those prayers which differ in the two rites were recited silently, and only the hymn sung after the commemoration of the Mother of God in the anaphora was both different and audible. Here we can notice briefly the main developments which brought the Liturgy to its final form.

The Preparation of the Clergy

From the eleventh century onwards various devotions for the clergy to say on entering the church appear in the euchologia, the collections of prayers needed by the priest in the course of the different services. They increased in number and diversity as time went on. Later, perhaps not before the fourteenth century, prayers were provided to be said before the icons of the Christ Pantocrator and the Mother of God in the iconostasis, and on entering the sanctuary. The washing of hands, which by this time had been transferred in a presbyteral Liturgy from its old place after the Great Entrance to the preliminary rites of the service, was also accompanied by prayers and psalms. These devotions, in which there was a good deal of variety, may not to begin with have been obligatory. They were in essence formalizations of natural clerical devotion: but their inclusion in the text of the Liturgy heightened its increasingly clerical flavour.

Prayers accompanying the vesting of the clergy appeared first in the thirteenth century, and soon a prayer was provided for each item of vesture. The originally secular dress of the clergy had, since its abandonment by the laity from the sixth century in favour of newer styles, become distinctively ecclesiastical: the linea became the stikharion, or alb; the paenula became the phelonion, or chasuble, and from the eleventh century was decorated with many crosses, and called the polystavrion. In the later Byzantine period the clergy adopted further items of secular dress. Patriarchs took to wearing the imperial sakkos – not unlike the western dalmatic in appearance – and epimanikia, or cuffs. Their use spread to senior bishops, and after the fall of Constantinople to all bishops. The cuffs were adopted by priests, and eventually by deacons too. By a similar process the imperial mitre became the normal head-dress of the bishops in church. The Orthodox Church preserved something of the outward panoply of the Byzantine Empire after its political disappearance, and in the vested bishop the appearance of the Byzantine Emperor lived on. The vesting prayers reflected the symbolic significance which had come to be attached to each article of liturgical clothing.

The Prothesis, or Proskomidia

The proskomidia in the *Diataxis* is almost identical with the present form. One difference of interest is that the deacon too cuts out particles, in commemoration of himself, and any of the living and departed he wishes to pray for, and places them on the paten, 'as the priest does'. It is the last remnant of the original role of the deacon in the preparation of the gifts.

By now the birth-symbolism of Nicholas of Andida has given rise to an appropriate action. When the preparation of the paten is complete, a star-shaped frame is put over it to support the covering veil. The priest censes it and says as he puts it in place: 'And the star came and stood over where the young child was'. In text as in interpretation, the proskomidia now symbolizes both passion and death, and birth.

Philotheos prescribes the censing of the altar and sanctuary, and of the nave, once the preparation of the gifts is over. The first mention of such preliminary censing by the deacon as a regular part of the Liturgy occurs in the thirteenth century, though it was occasionally done much earlier, and was mentioned by Dionysius the Areopagite as part of the Syrian rite at the end of the fifth century. As he censes the altar the deacon says the troparion 'In the grave with the body . . .', a text attracted to this point of the service by the symbolic association of the altar with the tomb of Christ.

The Little Entrance

By the fourteenth century the book of the Gospels had come to be kept on the altar. The Little Entrance, now so called, was therefore a purely symbolic procession, for it began where it was to end, in the sanctuary. Only at an episcopal Liturgy did something of its origin as the entrance of the bishop into the church remain.

The chant sung at the entrance, 'O come, let us worship and fall down before Christ', is the remains of the old third antiphon, which also served to cover the entry. From the eleventh century its original refrain, 'Only-begotten Son' had been transferred to the second antiphon, and the present refrains were used. At the same time additional troparia began to be sung, enabling other aspects of the feast or additional commemorations to be included. Two or three were sung in the twelfth century, three in the thirteenth. After the fourteenth century the number increased still further.

The Readings

Germanos had spoken of incense after his comment on the Alleluia, without saying anything about its use. In origin it was no doubt used to reverence the Gospel-book, understood as a symbol of Christ the living Word of God. By the eleventh century the altar was sometimes censed as well as the book, and the censing gradually expanded, taking in the clergy, the sanctuary and the prothesis, and eventually the iconostasis and the congregation. It was originally performed during the Alleluia and the psalm to which it was the refrain. But its expansion, and the devotions prescribed for the deacon before the reading of the Gospel, left insufficient time for it then. So it came to be begun during the first reading. Philotheos says it may be done at either point. Performed during the reading, it tended to transfer attention from one of the primary elements in the service to a secondary.

The Great Entrance

Several developments had taken place since the eleventh century which deserve to be noticed.

First, priests now regularly take part in the procession. No doubt when there were no deacons, or only one, priests had of necessity to help bring in the gifts and other necessities. But as early as the tenth century priests sometimes carried them in even when a deacon was present. In time all the clergy, with the exception of the bishop, took part even when they had nothing to carry: though the number of accessories connected with the Entrance ensured that at least some of them had something to bring in. Fans, spear, spoon, paten and chalice veils, and the aer, were all carried in the procession, in addition to the bread on the paten and the chalice of wine and water. Perhaps it was the great solemnity with which the Entrance was performed that attracted into the procession all available clergy, so in part at any rate depriving the deacons of one of their traditional functions.

By its splendour and solemnity the procession of the Great Entrance so dominated the Liturgy that it is entirely understandable that in iconography it could stand for the whole Liturgy. Despite the warning of Patriarch Euthymius, popular devotions at the Entrance continued to verge on the excessive, and Nicholas Cabasilas found it necessary to emphasize that the gifts were not yet consecrated. People prostrated themselves to reverence the gifts, and asked the prayers of the clergy. They lay down in front of the procession, so that the clergy had to step over them; and they sought to be touched by the sacred vessels.

Second, commemorations were made during the procession. Philotheos prescribes one general commemoration: 'May the Lord God remember all of us in his kingdom.' It was made quietly, without interrupting the Cherubic Hymn. The priest made it in response to the people's request for his prayers, which was one of the ways in which they could associate themselves with the Liturgy. He might repeat it several times as he moved through the church. It was an informal commemoration to begin with, exactly similar to the commemoration of each other which the clergy made as they entered the sanctuary.

The earliest reference to the custom dates from the twelfth or thirteenth century. By the middle of the fourteenth century the Emperor and the patriarch were commemorated when they took part in the service. But these commemorations were also made silently on other occasions, and so were those of other individuals or orders as they came to be added. By the fifteenth century the general commemoration was coming to be made out loud, at first after the Great Entrance, together with that of any important persons present at the Liturgy. Only later did commemorations made out loud multiply, so as to interrupt the singing of the Cherubicon and divide it into two.

A third development concerned the deposition of the gifts on the altar. It seems that originally whoever had carried in the paten and chalice put them on the altar. By the thirteenth century the priest was beginning to take them from the deacon, when the latter brought them in, and set them on the altar. At an episcopal Liturgy the bishop did so. It was another instance of liturgical functions passing from a lower to a higher order in the hierarchy.

By the fourteenth century, too, the interpretation of this necessary act as symbolizing the burial of Christ had given rise to an appropriate text. Philotheos directs the priest to say the troparion 'Noble Joseph'. This was originally sung in the procession with the epitaphios representing the burial of Christ, which was added in the fourteenth century to the end of Matins on Holy Saturday. It was apparently from here that it passed into the Liturgy. Later other troparia were added to it, relating to different aspects of Christ's death, burial and resurrection, and drawn from the offices of Good Friday, Holy Saturday and Eastertide.

A large number of other formulae came to be added to the Great Entrance at various points, including Psalm 51, the creed, the Lord's Prayer, and the Trisagion, to mention but a few. They did not all find a permanent place, and were all, like most of the additions to the text of the service at this stage, purely clerical devotions which in no way affected the public rite.

The Anaphora and Communion

Among the issues hotly debated between Orthodox and Latin Catholics was the precise moment of consecration in the Eucharist. The Western tradition had for centuries associated it with the narrative, and later more narrowly with the precise words, of institution. The Eastern had come more and more to link it with the invocation of the Holy Spirit. Since the matter became one of contention, each side had tended to become more intransigent. The Orthodox view led to greater liturgical emphasis on the epiclesis. Philotheos directs the deacon to bow his head slightly and to point to the paten with his stole, saying: 'Bless, master, the holy bread'. The priest makes the sign of the cross over the bread as he says: 'And make this bread the precious Body of your Christ'. When the chalice has been similarly blessed, the deacon says 'Amen, Amen', and makes three reverences. In some churches a devotional invocation of the Spirit, used in Lent at the Third Hour, came to be said by the clergy before the liturgical epiclesis.

The Communion of the clergy was prescribed in detail by Philotheos, and included various devotions. The *Diataxis* recognizes that there might be no lay communicants at all. However much frequent Communion might have been held out as an ideal, the laity had for long communicated no more than once or twice a year, and in time reception of Communion became a matter for congratulation even in monastic circles.

The Interpretation of the Liturgy

The Byzantine tradition of liturgical exposition culminated in two writers, each of whom finally tied up one of the two threads of which that tradition was woven. In his great *Commentary on the Divine Liturgy* the fourteenth-century lay theologian Nicholas Cabasilas retains the interpretation of the rite, stemming from the Antiochene school, as a symbolic representation of the historic life of Jesus Christ. Unlike Nicholas of Andida, he applies the principle with discretion and moderation, insisting on the primary significance of the prayers, readings and actions which make up the service. Above all he is clear as to the essentially sacramental nature of the commemoration of Christ in the Eucharist, and of the centrality of Communion to the meaning of the Liturgy. There is little doubt that Cabasilas' *Commentary* embodies a deliberate reaction against the exaggerated use of symbolism in Nicholas of Andida's work.

In the following century Symeon, a monk who became Archbishop of Thessalonike in 1416/17 and died in 1429, wrote two treatises. An earlier *Interpretation of the Church and the Liturgy* was followed by *On the Holy Liturgy*. Though he had apparently read Cabasilas' work, he was little influenced by it. He regarded himself as one of the last of the disciples of Dionysius the Areopagite, and wrote from within the Alexandrian tradition represented by Maximus the Confessor.

Cabasilas' *Commentary on the Divine Liturgy*

Little is known of the author of what is perhaps the greatest of all the Byzantine expositions of the Liturgy, which can still be read with considerable profit. He enjoyed a reputation for both theological learning and holiness of life, and his portrait was painted in the church of the Protaton in Karyes on Mount Athos. He wrote too a treatise on *The Life in Christ*, in which he roots the mystical life of Christians firmly in the sacramental rites of the Church. His *Commentary on the Liturgy* presupposes the fully-developed rite much as Philotheos describes it.

Cabasilas' firm grasp of the basic meaning of the Liturgy emerges at the very beginning:

> The essential act in the celebration of the holy mysteries in the transformation of the elements into the divine Body and Blood; its aim is the sanctification of the faithful, who through these mysteries receive the remission of their sins and the inheritance of the Kingdom of heaven. As a preparation for, and contribution to, this act and for this purpose, we have prayers, psalms, and readings from the holy Scripture: in short, all the sacred acts and forms which are said and done before and after the consecration of the elements.

By their actual content, 'all these things, which make the souls of both priest and people better and more divine, make them fit for the reception and preservation of the holy mysteries'. But

> there is another way in which these forms, like all the ceremonies of the holy sacrifice, sanctify us. It consists in this, that in them Christ and the deeds he accomplished and the sufferings he endured for our sakes are represented. Indeed, it is the whole scheme of the work of redemption which is signified in the psalms and readings, as in all the actions of the priest throughout the Liturgy: the first ceremonies of the service represent the beginnings of this work, the next, the sequel, and the last, its results. Thus those who are present at these ceremonies have before their eyes all these divine things.

But Cabasilas is quite clear that the essential commemoration of Christ is sacramental and real, not symbolic:

> The consecration of the elements – the sacrifice itself – commemorates the death, resurrection, and ascension of the Saviour, since it transforms these precious gifts into the very Body of the Lord, that body which was the central figure in all these mysteries, which was crucified, which rose from the dead, which ascended into heaven.

159

So he underlines the fundamental importance of the anaphora and the consecration of the gifts, which earlier commentators, concentrating on their symbolic interpretations, had tended to pass over, or at best to reduce to the same level of symbolic significance as the rest of the service.

At the same time Cabasilas defends the legitimacy of adding symbolic significance to the natural and primary function of the different parts of the rite:

> Even if one maintains that the readings and psalms serve another purpose – for they were introduced in order to dispose us to virtue and to cause God to look favourably on us – that does not mean that the same ceremonies cannot at once urge us to virtue and illustrate the scheme of Christ's redemptive work. Robes fulfil their function as clothes and cover the body; but sometimes by their style they indicate the profession, rank and dignity of the wearer. The same is true of these liturgical matters. Because the holy Scriptures contain divinely inspired words and praises of God, and because they incite to virtue, they sanctify those who read or chant them. But because of the selection which has been made, and the order in which the passages have been arranged, they have another function: they signify the coming of Christ and his work. Not only the chants and readings, but the very actions themselves have this part to play. Each has its own immediate purpose and usefulness. But at the same time each symbolizes some part of the works of Christ, his deeds or his sufferings. For example, we have the bringing of the Gospel to the altar, then the bringing of the offerings. Each is done for a purpose, the one that the Gospel may be read, the other that the sacrifice may be performed. Besides this, however, one represents the appearance and the other the manifestation of the Saviour; the first, obscure and imperfect, at the beginning of his life, the second, the perfect and supreme manifestation. There are even certain ceremonies which fulfil no practical purpose, but have only a figurative meaning.

This symbolic presentation of God's plan of salvation enables us to contemplate his love and mercy, and so be moved to renew our faith, devotion and love. The Liturgy is meant to affect us not only at the level of conscious thought: it is meant to appeal also to our emotions, so that we can respond to God's love with our whole being. The worshipper is invited to see, as well as to think about, the love of God revealed in Jesus Christ, and through contemplation of it to be sanctified. But contemplation as a means of sanctification is subordinate to the reception of the mysteries:

> Filled with these ideas, and with their memory fresh within us, we participate in the holy mysteries. In this way, adding sanctification to sanctification, that of the sacred rite to that of contemplation, we are changed from glory to glory, that is to say, from the lesser to that which is greatest of all.

Commenting on the proskomidia, Cabasilas explains that there is a preliminary preparation of the gifts because Christ was offered to God from the very beginning of his life, although he was sacrificed only at its close. The removal of the portion to be consecrated from the first prosphora indicates that Christ was separated from the mass of humankind to be a sacrifice. He combines the older passion-symbolism of the proskomidia with the more recent birth-symbolism, teaching that what is done to represent the passion is a prophetic dramatization of Christ's sufferings and death, which had been foretold in the Old Testament. Christ was born in order to die.

Cabasilas stresses that the bread remains bread so long as it is in the prothesis: he was concerned to discourage the popular view that the gifts were already the objects of veneration. He sums up the meaning of the proskomidia in this way:

> The words and actions performed over the bread which signify the death of the Lord are only a description and a symbol. The bread therefore remains bread and has received no more than a capacity to be offered to God. That is why it typifies the Lord's body in his early years, for, as we have already pointed out, he himself was an offering from his birth onwards. This is why the priest relates, and represents over the bread, the miracles accomplished in him when he was but new born and still lying in the manger.

These include the placing of the asteriskos and the veiling of the gifts. He concludes: 'Thus the power of the incarnate God was veiled up to the time of his miracles and witness from heaven. But those who know say of him: "The Lord has reigned, clothed in beauty", and the other passages which imply his divinity'.

A short treatise on Christian prayer, and a lengthy exposition of the meaning of peace – incorporating the basic teaching of the Eastern Christian tradition on the need to acquire stillness, hesychia – preface Cabasilas' explanation of the first part of the service. The three antiphons, taken from the prophetic writings, represent the time before John the Baptist, and are prophetic testimonies to the coming of Christ and his achievements. This time comes to an end with the raising of the Gospel-book at the Little Entrance, which symbolizes the manifestation of Christ to the multitudes. The union of heaven and earth, effected by the incarnation, is reflected in the prayer of the Little Entrance, and in the Trisagion. The Church on earth sings the song of the angels, for now angels and men form one Church, a single choir, since Christ was of both heaven and earth.

The scripture readings, apart from their practical purpose, represent the manifestation of the Saviour soon after his showing, when he 'mingled with the crowd and made himself known not only by his own words, but also by that which he taught to his apostles in sending them to the lost sheep of the house of Israel'. The Gospel is read after the Epistle, although historically it should be the other way round, 'because that which our Lord himself said constitutes a more perfect manifestation than the words of the apostles'.

Commenting on the Great Entrance, Cabasilas again insists on the practical as well as the symbolic significance of the procession:

> The priest ... comes to the altar of the prothesis, takes the offerings, and reverently holding them head-high, departs. Carrying them thus, he goes to the altar, after walking in slow and solemn procession through the nave of the church. The faithful chant during the procession, kneeling down reverently and devoutly, and praying that they may be remembered when the offering is made. The priest goes on, surrounded by candles and incense, until he comes to the altar. This is done, no doubt, for practical reasons; it was necessary to bring the offerings which are to be sacrificed to the altar and set them down there, and to do this with all reverence and devotion ... Also this ceremony signifies the last manifestation of Christ, which aroused the hatred of the Jews, when he embarked on the journey from his native country to Jerusalem, where he was to be sacrificed: then he rode into the holy city on the back of an ass, escorted by a cheering crowd.

He goes on to describe how the people must prostrate themselves, and ask for the prayers of the priest: for intercession at the

Eucharist is particularly efficacious. Cabasilas' language here is reminiscent of that of Cyril of Jerusalem, and shows how the latter's view of the Eucharist as a propitiatory sacrifice had become an integral part of the Orthodox tradition. His warning to the faithful not to confuse the Great Entrance in the ordinary Liturgy with that in the Liturgy of the Presanctified, when alone devotion to the gifts as consecrated is justified, testifies to the persistence of popular devotion at this point from the time of Theodore of Mopsuestia onward, deriving perhaps less from a confusion between the two Liturgies than from the perceived implications of the splendour with which the transfer of the gifts had been attended since that time, and which the development of the proskomidia had only served to reinforce.

Cabasilas' comments on the exclamation, 'The doors! The doors!', is of some interest in illustrating the curious development of liturgical practice and symbolism at this point. Originally a command to close the doors of the church, it came to be understood as an injunction to close those of the sanctuary. But by the fourteenth century these were open during the saying of the creed. So Cabasilas relates it to our need to open our mouths and ears in the wisdom we have learnt through our faith in God.

The commentary on the anaphora is theological: for its function is to change the gifts into the Body and Blood of the Lord, and so to effect the commemoraticn of his passion, death and resurrection. Here symbolism gives way to reality. The most important parts of the prayer are the institution narrative and the epiclesis. Following the tradition which goes back to Cyril of Jerusalem, Cabasilas sees the whole rite accomplished once the words of the epiclesis have been prayed:

> When these words have been said, the whole sacred rite is accomplished, the offerings are consecrated, the sacrifice complete, the divine oblation, slain for the salvation of the world, lies upon the altar. For it is no longer the bread, which until now has represented the Lord's Body, nor is it a simple offering, bearing the likeness of the true offering, carrying as if engraved on it the symbols of the Saviour's passion: it is the true victim, the most holy Body of the Lord, which really suffered the outrages, insults, and blows, which was crucified and slain, which under Pontius Pilate bore such splendid witness; that body which was mocked, scourged, spat upon, and which tasted gall. In like manner the wine has become the

Blood which flowed from that body. It is that Body and Blood formed by the Holy Spirit, born of the Virgin Mary, which was buried, which rose again on the third day, which ascended into heaven and sits down at the right hand of the Father.

After a lengthy defence of the Orthodox theology of consecration, and an exposition of the nature of the eucharistic sacrifice, Cabasilas completes his explanation of the Liturgy. The only further detail to which he attaches symbolic significance is the zeon: the hot water put into the chalice before Communion symbolizes the descent of the Holy Spirit on the Church, which 'comes about when the sacrifice has been offered and the holy offerings have reached their perfection; it will be completed in those who communicate worthily'.

Symeon of Thessalonike

In order to take part in the Liturgy fully, according to Symeon, it is necessary to understand the meaning of what is done in the course of its celebration. For it is made up of symbols which contain a hidden reality – Symeon adopts Dionysius' understanding of a symbol. But properly understood liturgical symbols reveal two different orders of reality. First and foremost they set before the worshipper the whole saving economy of God in Christ: his voluntary humiliation in his incarnation, passion and death; and his resurrection and glorification. The Liturgy at the same time fulfils the Old Testament prefigurations of Christ, and anticipates the ultimate reality of the heavenly Kingdom.

But contemplation of the liturgical rites also gives access to a spiritual reality, which is Christ, considered less in his incarnate economy than as the eternal Word of God. As the human spirit is purified it receives from God the gift of illumination, which enables it to ascend from the material symbols to the spiritual reality they contain. It thus advances in understanding towards the perfect knowledge of the mysteries which is the goal of the Christian life. Symeon views this progress in the same hierarchical way as Dionysius: each of the heavenly and earthly orders mediates knowledge of the mysteries to those below it. But he differs from the Areopagite in setting contemplation of the mysteries firmly within the historic economy of redemption.

In his work *On the Church and the Liturgy* Symeon claims only to be following the holy fathers, from whom he has derived his interpretation. His remarks reveal the extent to which tradition had come to dominate Byzantine and Orthodox thought and practice. Symeon's work is the final consolidation of the tradition of liturgical interpretation, and reflects the assumption that the Liturgy had always been as it was in the fifteenth century:

For we have not added anything new to what has been handed on, nor have we changed what we have received. But we have preserved them, as we do the symbol of faith. We celebrate the Liturgy as it has been given to us by the Saviour and the apostles and the fathers. And as the Lord celebrated with his disciples, and broke the bread and gave it to them and likewise the chalice, so the church does, the bishop celebrating with the priests, or the priest with other priests. The successor of the apostles, I mean the holy Dionysius, witnesses to this, teaching how to celebrate, as we do. And Basil and Chrysostom, who taught divine things, expounding more largely the order of the mystagogy, handed it down to be performed as our church performs it, and their prayers in the Liturgy testify, teaching the first and second entries, and the rest of the holy rite.

Symeon first deals with the church building, for which by this time a developed rite of consecration existed:

The church, although it is composed of material things, has grace from on high: for it is consecrated by the mystical prayers of the bishop, and anointed with sacred oil, and is wholly the dwelling of God. Not everyone can go everywhere in it: some parts are for the priests, some for the laity.

The division of the church into two – nave and sanctuary – or three, if the narthex is included, has multiple meaning:

The fact that it has two parts, sanctuary and nave, represents Christ, who is both God and man, the one invisible, the other visible. Similarly it represents man, who is both soul and body. But especially it signifies the mystery of the Trinity, which is inaccessible in its essence, but known in its providence and powers. In particular it represents the visible world and the invisible, and also the visible world only: the heavens by the holy sanctuary, things on earth by the holy nave. From another point of view the whole of the church can be seen as threefold: the parts in front of the nave, the nave, and the sanctuary. This signifies the Trinity, and the heavenly orders arranged in

165

threes; and the pious people divided into three, I mean, the priests, the perfect believers, and the penitents. But the pattern of the holy church also teaches the things on earth and in heaven, and those above the heavens: the narthex, what is on the earth; the nave, the things in heaven; the holy sanctuary, what is above the heavens.

The chancel barrier signifies the distinction between sensible and spiritual realities, and the sanctuary curtain represents the heavenly tabernacle of God. The stone altar points us to Christ as the rock: its under-cover represents the grave clothes, the rich top cover symbolizes his glory. The incense represents the fragrant grace of the Holy Spirit, the lighted candles the illumination given by the Spirit. The ambo symbolizes the stone rolled over the entrance to the tomb. All the adornments of the church represent the beauty of creation: the lights imitate the stars, the corona (of lights) the firmament.

When he comes to the clergy, Symeon follows Dionysius in understanding their different orders as representing the angelic orders in heaven. To this he adds a detailed symbolic interpretation of their vestments, giving also the prayer formula which was said when they were put on. The priests are an image of the first choir of angels, the deacons, readers and chanters represent the middle choir. The bishop is the image of Christ himself, and is the source of all illumination in the church. Symeon explains in his work *On the Holy Liturgy* that his vestments consist of seven items, corresponding to the seven gifts of the Spirit. At this time it was still only senior bishops who wore the imperial sakkos: others still wore the polystavrion, the phelonion covered with crosses. The priest wears five items, corresponding to the five senses, and the five powers of the soul, which the priest sanctifies by his sacramental ministry. The deacon has only two items to put on. The prayer formulae Symeon cites are those of the present Liturgy.

In his *Interpretation of the Church and the Liturgy* Symeon does not speak of the proskomidia. At the end of the work he apologizes for this omission, saying that since the fathers had already written about it there was no need for him to do so. In fact the prothesis as interpreted by Nicholas of Andida and Cabasilas did not fit in well with Symeon's basic scheme, taken from Maximus the Confessor, in whose time there was no proskomidia. But he does include it in *On the Holy Liturgy*, where he presupposes the same form as Cabasilas, and ascribes to it a similar twofold symbolic meaning, reconciling birth- and passion-symbolism in the same way: the latter is prophetic of what will be accomplished later.

Symeon sees in the use of leavened bread a symbol of the perfect humanity of Christ. The leaven represents his human soul, the salt his spirit. The water represents baptism. After attacking both Latins and Armenians, he goes on to describe the cutting out of the commemorative particles. They are not consecrated in the Liturgy, but are only gifts and sacrifices. But because they are so close on the paten to the Lamb which is consecrated, they bring sanctification to those for whom they are offered. Put into the chalice, they effect a kind of spiritual communion, which can bring profit or condemnation to the soul of the person concerned, depending on his spiritual condition.

Describing the final stages of the proskomidia, Symeon attacks the practice of deacons also offering particles, which Philotheos had allowed; they can do so only through the priests. In Thessalonike he had put a stop to this practice, still current on Mount Athos. His objection stems from his hierarchical view of the ministry, in which the inferior orders can do nothing without the permission of their superior.

Coming to the Liturgy itself, Symeon comments on an episcopal celebration, in which the original structure of the rite is less obscured than in a presbyteral Liturgy. Ready vested in the sanctuary the bishop 'having put on the sacred vestments signifies the holy incarnation'. When he descends from his throne in the apse, 'he is an image of the condescension of the Word of God to us'. 'Going to the doors of the holy church, he shows forth his coming on earth and manifestation, and his descent to death and Hades. This is what his going to the west means. The holy Liturgy begins when the bishop gives the sign, for nothing can be done without him. The priests who are saying the prayers within (the sanctuary) typify the heavenly orders.'

Meanwhile the antiphons are being sung. Since the psalms represent the prophets who foretold the coming of Christ, they symbolize the incarnation and the work of the incarnate Word for us. The bishop remains in the nave, accompanied by the deacons who 'not only represent the apostles, but the angels, who were ministering to him in his mysteries'.

When the priests within the sanctuary have finished the

prayers, and have come out, they represent the coming down of the holy angels at the resurrection and ascension of Christ. Then the bishop, bowing his head together with the priests, prays that the angels might enter with them and celebrate with them. In bowing his head and raising it he manifests the resurrection of the Lord. The deacon too proclaims this, raising the Gospel-book, announcing the resurrection of the Saviour and exclaiming in a loud voice: 'Wisdom! Stand upright', witnessing to the resurrection in word and deed. After this there is at once the image of the ascension: candles going before, deacons leading the way in pairs, the holy Gospel-book being held, the bishop himself being supported by deacons, the other priests following after.

Since the nave represents earth, and the sanctuary heaven, the bishop's entry into the sanctuary visibly signifies Christ's exaltation.

The censing of the altar that follows represents the coming of the Spirit, which completes the revelation of the Trinity. Appropriately therefore the Trisagion is now sung, both by those in the sanctuary and those in the nave: for through the incarnation of Christ 'there has come to be one church of angels and men'. Going to his throne the bishop 'witnesses to Christ's sitting at the right hand of the Father', while his blessing with the trikirion (the triple candlestick) 'confirms for us the sanctification which comes from the Trinity'.

The reading of the apostolic words signifies the mission of the apostles to the Gentiles, while that of the Gospel 'manifests the proclamation of the gospel in all the world which was made by the disciples'. After that comes the end, the time of the consummation, represented by the dismissal of the catechumens. The final coming of Christ is symbolized by the Great Entrance, whose proper splendour Symeon emphasizes:

> After this the escorting and entrance of the venerable gifts takes place with splendour, readers, deacons and priests with the holy vessels going before and following, because this represents the final coming of Christ, as we have said, when he will come with glory. Wherefore the omophorion with the cross on it comes in front, which displays the sign of Jesus about to appear from heaven, and represents Jesus himself. With it come the other deacons, signifying the angelic orders. Then come those who bear the holy gifts, followed by all the

others, and those who carry the holy epitaphios on their heads, depicting Jesus naked and dead.

At this time the epitaphios, now used only in Holy Week, served as the aer to cover all the vessels on the altar. Its iconography expressed the interpretation of the deposition of the gifts as symbolic of the burial of Christ. The prayer which the priests make as they go through the church, in response to the people's requests for prayer, shows that when the end comes our inheritance is none other than the Kingdom of God – 'May the Lord God remember you in his Kingdom.'

Popular devotion at the Great Entrance found a more willing protagonist in Symeon than it had in Cabasilas. He holds that veneration of the gifts is perfectly justified, since they are already images of the Body and Blood of Christ, comparable to, though greater than, icons. They are, as St Basil called them, antitypes of the Body and Blood of Christ, and have already been offered to become the Body and Blood. Symeon reckons worse than iconoclasts those who criticize such veneration as idolatry. He encourages the veneration even of holy vessels which are empty, 'for they all partake of sanctification, the holy gifts being offered in sacrifice in them'. Perhaps Symeon was deliberately trying to correct what he considered Cabasilas' mistaken caution. But his use of the word antitype is significant, for in the anaphora of St Basil it is used of the consecrated gifts. Symeon here reflects the view by now deeply ingrained in Orthodox eucharistic piety, that a certain holiness attaches to the bread and wine from the time of their preparation in the prothesis. This is in fact implied by the prayers said during the proskomidia, and by the ceremonial surrounding both that rite and the Great Entrance. The function of the anaphora as the prayer which offers the gifts to God and so prays for their consecration had come to be anticipated in their preliminary preparation. To justify what had become unquestionable traditional practice a distinction had to be drawn between offering the gifts – in the proskomidia – and offering them in sacrifice – in the anaphora. Symeon provided a theological justification for an attitude which Cabasilas, the better liturgical theologian, saw could not be defended without detracting from the essential meaning and centrality of the eucharistic prayer.

Following Maximus the Confessor, Symeon has now exhausted the possibility of attaching events in the history of salvation to particular parts of the Liturgy: there is nothing to be added after the second coming. But half of the service has yet to take place. Maximus, as we have seen, comments only on the kiss of peace, the creed, the Sanctus, and the Lord's Prayer. Symeon now adopts the alternative scheme of interpretation of Germanos and Nicholas of Andida, which fits awkwardly with that of Maximus, since it entails a return to earlier stages in the life of Christ. So the covering of the gifts on the altar after the Great Entrance indicates that Jesus was not recognized by all at the beginning, and that the incarnation did not detract from his divinity. He is in fact always incomprehensible and infinite, and is only known in so far as he reveals himself.

At the same time much of what follows is an expression of present and anticipated spiritual realities. The kiss of peace is given 'because we have been united by the right confession of the Trinity and the incarnation of one of the Trinity, and this confession has united us with the angels'. It also reminds us that we must love one another, because Christ offered himself in sacrifice because of love, and that all will be friends in the age to come. To that age too the Sanctus points, for then 'we shall give equal praise with the angels and be united with them'.

Symeon offers a concise description of the content of the anaphora after the Sanctus, and stresses the reality of the presence of the Body and Blood of Christ, and so of 'living delight and infinite joy and the Kingdom of heaven' set forth on the holy table for everyone. This present reality has yet to be consummated, however, and the Lord's Prayer 'is a sign of our future union with God in the Holy Spirit through the only-begotten Son, when we shall be sons of God through adoption and grace'. But he reverts to another tradition when he says that the elevation of the bread represents the elevation of Jesus on the cross, and that in the bread the bishop contemplates Jesus crucified. The breaking of the bread has already signified what Jesus did at the Last Supper: and the adding of hot water to the chalice shows that the body of Jesus remained life-giving even after death. After Communion, which points to our indissoluble union with Jesus in the age to come, the censing of the gifts and their transfer to the prothesis symbolizes the ascension of the Lord, and the proclamation of the gospel in all the world.

The antidoron is received by those who have not communicated. It is not the Communion of the Body of Christ, but it is sanctified, having been signed with the lance and received the holy words, and so is properly called the antidoron, 'because it gives the gift of God's grace'.

Symeon brought together in his interpretation of the Liturgy all the strands which he found in earlier expressions of Byzantine liturgical exposition. Those strands, as we have seen, belonged to two main traditions of interpretation, which might seem to be alternative rather than complementary. But the Byzantine mind was capable of combining them into a complex, if not always consistent, pattern of liturgical exposition, which became after Symeon's synthesis part of the unquestioned heritage of the Orthodox Christian tradition.

9 Epilogue

Nicholas Cabasilas and Symeon of Thessalonike commented on a Liturgy whose development had in all essentials come to an end. Since their day the Liturgy has changed little. Celebrated by all Orthodox Christians in the same way, with only minor variations in practice, each Church using its own liturgical language, it is one of the bonds which unites the autocephalous Orthodox Churches into one family. With the other services of the Church, it is the expression in prayer and worship of the faith which they hold in common, and which is the other main bond holding them together. Just as the tradition of faith, set forth by the Fathers of the fourth to eighth centuries, is held to be the authoritative expression of Orthodox belief, so the liturgical tradition, which in its main lines and much of its content was laid down in the same period, is considered the enduring expression of Orthodox worship.

The inherent conservatism which increasingly characterized the Byzantine Church from the eighth century onwards was inherited in full measure by the Slav Churches founded from Constantinople. It was reinforced by external circumstances. From the time of the Arab Muslim conquest of the territory of the ancient Patriarchates of Alexandria, Antioch and Jerusalem in the early seventh century, the Orthodox Churches found themselves increasingly under non-Christian rule. By the time Constantinople fell to the Turks in 1453, the Eastern Roman Empire consisted of little more than the city itself. Most of south-east Europe was already within the Ottoman Empire, and by the end of the fifteenth century only the two Romanian principalities of Moldavia and Wallachia maintained a precarious independence, before finally becoming tributary to the Sublime Porte in Istanbul. Only in Muscovite Russia did the Orthodox Church live in a Christian state, which had itself only recently succeeded in freeing itself from two centuries of Tatar domination.

Such historical circumstances laid upon the Orthodox Churches a twofold responsibility. Bearers of the Christian tradition to their peoples, they became the bearers of their peoples' sense of national identity under often oppressive rule.

Where the Church could do little but worship in church buildings, the Liturgy became the expression of more than Christian
religious devotion. The need to preserve national as well as
Christian tradition tended to foster a still stronger conservatism
in all aspects of church life. Modern history has done little to
change the situation for most Orthodox Christians. The Orthodox Church in Russia had not had time to profit from its new-
found freedom from imperial control and from the restoration of
the patriarchate in 1917 before it fell under the rule of an
officially atheist state. Most of the Churches of south-east Europe
had less than a century of freedom from Ottoman rule before they
too found themselves after the Second World War obliged to live
within the restrictions imposed by officially Marxist states. Only
in Greece does a major Orthodox Church live in an officially
Orthodox Christian country. The growing Orthodox Churches
in the West are for the most part still closely related to their
mother Churches in traditionally Orthodox countries. Drawing
their membership largely from Orthodox from those countries
living in diaspora, with some local converts to Orthodoxy, they
are often under quite strong pressure to conserve and pass on the
national Orthodox culture from which they originate.

It is not surprising, therefore, that the Orthodox Churches
have so far experienced nothing resembling the so-called liturgical movement which has so affected contemporary worship in the
Western Churches. That movement springs from several different sources in the modern development of Western Christianity. The study of the history of Western Christian worship has
led to the realization that the forms of service which by the
present century had become traditional, and the way in which
they were celebrated, had been influenced by trends similar to
those we have seen at work in the development of the Orthodox
Liturgy. Some of the basic principles of early Christian worship,
and in particular of eucharistic worship, had been overlaid and
obscured by later developments. At the same time the study of
the New Testament and of the doctrine of the Church has led to
the recovery of an understanding of the Church as a believing,
worshipping and witnessing community, rather than as a clericalized institution providing religious activities for a relatively
passive laity. So the celebration of the Eucharist has come to be
seen as the characteristic action of the Christian community,
celebrated by the whole people of God exercising the royal
priesthood conferred on it by God in baptism. From this cele-

bration flows the active witness and service of the Christian community in the life of the world – what an Orthodox writer has called 'the Liturgy after the Liturgy'.

These perceptions, which underlie the renewal of liturgical worship in the Western Christian traditions, are certainly not lacking within the Orthodox Church. In particular Alexander Schmemann articulated them forcefully in his book *Introduction to Liturgical Theology*. There he points critically to those developments in the Byzantine Liturgy which made it less and less a celebration of the whole Church, and increasingly a clericalized act for the satisfaction of individual Christian religious needs. He is critical, too, of the tradition of symbolic interpretation of the Liturgy, which obscured the essentially sacramental character of the Eucharist. Schmemann's analysis of the development of the Liturgy is based on the same perceptions which have inspired the liturgical movement in Western Churches. But the Orthodox Churches live for the most part in circumstances so different from those of Western Christians that there is no present possibility of, nor indeed any desire for, a reform of Orthodox worship similar to the Western movement of renewal.

That does not mean that no changes at all are taking place in the celebration of the Liturgy in the Orthodox Churches. In the Soviet Union and in other places, not least in the diaspora, many Orthodox receive Communion more frequently now than for many centuries. In Greek practice the litanies between the Gospel and the Great Entrance are normally omitted. In parish churches in Greece the Liturgy is normally celebrated with the royal doors open all the time, while some churches there, and many Greek churches in the United States of America, now have a much more open form of iconostasis. Some degree of visibility has been restored to the Liturgy for those in the nave. Some priests say at least part of the anaphora audibly, with perhaps one or two of the other prayers traditionally said 'mystically'. In some places, too, the people join in singing some parts of the service: the Trisagion, the creed, the Lord's Prayer, and perhaps some other chants. The tradition of symbolic interpretation of the Liturgy in terms of the historic life of Christ has not been formally abandoned, and as we have seen it is embodied to a certain extent in the text of the rite itself. But although it survives in a number of modern books on the Liturgy, it does so in a rather fragmented and attenuated form, and seems to have lost the vitality it once had. Such changes, however, do not amount to a

175

liturgical movement in the Western sense, and Western Christians generally perceive the Orthodox Liturgy as a traditional, conservative expression of eucharistic worship.

For some Western Christians that is one of the attractive characteristics of the Liturgy, as of Orthodoxy as a whole. Many religious people are inclined to be conservative, at least in the practice of their religion. The rapid process of change in ways of worship in Western Churches has not been welcomed with enthusiasm by all church members. The liturgical movement, as we saw in the first chapter, has encouraged emphasis to be laid on certain aspects of eucharistic worship. But there are others which have been neglected or even discouraged, whose importance is perhaps greater than contemporary Western liturgical fashion allows. Its conservative quality apart, there are several aspects of the Orthodox Liturgy from which Western Christians might usefully learn. Some of them are inevitably characteristics of all Orthodox worship, and not only of the Eucharist.

To begin with, there is the Orthodox understanding of the church building as itself sacramental. In Western tradition too churches are consecrated and set apart. But contemporary Western emphasis is on the Church as a holy community rather than on the church building as a holy place, and this influences the kind of building provided for worship. Yet these two emphases need not be mutually exclusive, and it can be a great help to prayerful worship to enter a place clearly understood and seen to be sacred space, enabling worshippers more easily to realize the presence of God and the communion of saints. This need be no escape from the world outside, but should be a reminder that the whole world of time and space is to be transfigured by God's grace into his Kingdom. The reality of that Kingdom is anticipated and experienced in the Eucharist, celebrated in the consecrated space of the church.

In the Orthodox Church icons are an integral part of that sacred space. Through them Christ, the Blessed Virgin Mary, the saints, and the whole economy of salvation are made visibly and sacramentally present to worshippers. The part icons can play in worship and prayer has begun to be appreciated among Western Christians, and one or two icons can quite often be found in churches. But the importance of icons and of the visual element in worship has still to be fully explored in the Western Churches. The Orthodox understanding of icons belongs in principle to the whole Church, for it was set forth by the Seventh Ecumenical

Council. But that Council was never fully understood or accepted in the West, and there is still much in the Orthodox tradition of iconography from which Western Christians can learn.

The use of the sense of sight in Orthodox worship is only one aspect of the way in which the Liturgy and other services draw the whole person into the prayer of the Church. All the senses and the entire body are involved. In front of the icons people light candles. The invariable use of incense at all services appeals to their sense of smell. Through their hearing music makes its appeal to them, for services are always sung or chanted, never read with the speaking voice. Icons, vestments and vessels may be touched and kissed; worshippers may be anointed or given blessed bread or other food to eat. They use their bodies in worship as they cross themselves at different moments in services, and bow or even prostrate themselves at appropriate moments. From this involvement of the whole person and all the senses Western Christians have much to learn. The Churches influenced by the Reformation have been traditionally suspicious of using the body or anything material in worship. They have separated spirit from matter, and in their emphasis on the word have appealed largely to the understanding and the intellect in worship. Recent reforms in the worship of all Western Churches have given renewed prominence to the verbal and intellectual content of services, while minimizing traditional aspects of liturgical worship and its setting which appealed to aspects of the human person other than the rational understanding. The conscious, reasoning mind must be involved in worship. But so must the senses and the emotions, and all that lies beneath the reasoning surface of human beings, for worship should draw into its Godward movement, and penetrate with God's sanctifying grace, the whole person.

Each whole person worships in relationship with other persons. It is the people of God which celebrates the Eucharist, and not a gathering of individuals unrelated to each other. But it is important that the relationship of the individual person to the community should be rightly conceived. There is an interesting, and perhaps important, difference in the way Orthodox and Western congregations behave in church in this respect. In reaction to the individualism which is held to have characterized much Western Christianity in recent centuries, Western Churches are concerned to emphasize the corporate nature of the Church and its worship. There is perhaps a danger of so stressing

177

its corporateness that individual persons are forced into an excessive conformity. Orthodox Christians have sometimes pointed out how regimented Western worshippers are, lined up in the rigid rows imposed by pewed, or chaired, churches. They are constrained by custom all to do the same thing at the same time. Such outward regimentation has not prevented inward individualism. But neither has the greater freedom given to Orthodox worshippers by the absence of pews or rows of chairs necessarily undermined a sense of worshipping as a community. At the same time the open space of the nave in an Orthodox church gives worshippers freedom to stand, kneel or prostrate themselves where they like, and to move about the church at appropriate times to venerate icons and light candles. Within a tradition which broadly prescribes how all present in church should behave, there is a degree of personal freedom surprising to Western worshippers. Perhaps this reflects a more balanced view of the relationship of individual Christians within the community than has so far been achieved in the Western Churches. The Church is neither a collection of individuals unrelated to each other, nor a collective in which the individual person is subordinated to the whole. It is a community of persons, sustaining each in their life in Christ, and sustained by all through their varied contributions. Perhaps the Orthodox Church, which has not experienced the individualism of Western European society and has therefore not known any reaction to it, can help the Western Churches to achieve the right balance between the two.

Christian community in the Church is both expressed and built up by sharing in Holy Communion at the Eucharist. There is a striking contrast between Orthodox and Western approaches to receiving Communion. It is now very unusual for Western Christians entitled to do so not to communicate at any celebration of the Eucharist they attend. They may even communicate twice in one day, if for some good reason they take part in two celebrations. The liturgical movement in the Roman Catholic and Anglican Churches, and the Parish Communion movement in the latter, have created a situation in which almost everyone receives Communion as a matter of course at the Sunday Eucharist. It is still unusual for many Orthodox Christians to communicate more than a few times in the year. In the serious preparation they traditionally undertake for Communion they resemble those reformed Churches in which Communion is also infrequent rather than contemporary Anglicans and Roman Catholics.

Epilogue

Occasional voices ask whether the return to general communion, where that has happened in the Western Churches, is all
gain. It is true that it is a return to early Christian practice. But it
is also true that the Church is not in the same situation as early
Christians: there is a greater diversity in degrees of commitment
now than then. Among Anglicans Archbishop Michael Ramsey,
writing some years ago in the context of a Church of England
where the Parish Communion was rapidly becoming the typical
Sunday service, drew attention to the risk of people receiving
Holy Communion too lightly. Serious preparation for Communion has largely disappeared, together with fasting for any
appreciable time before receiving. The rest of the service itself is
generally held to be sufficient preparation for its climax. But St
Paul's caution about the danger of eating and drinking at the
Eucharist 'without discerning the body' (1 Cor. 11.29) remains –
whatever interpretation may be given to that phrase. It cannot be
necessarily helpful either to the Church as a whole or to its
individual members that so little should be required in preparation for Communion. For participation in the Eucharist is not
only the sacrament of Christians' fellowship with one another in
the Body of Christ, but also and above all the sacrament of
Christians' communion with the holy God. The care with which
Orthodox receive the holy mysteries of Christ's Body and Blood
should at least raise a question for Western Christians about a
general Communion which may have become too easy.

That raises the issue of participation in worship. At most
celebrations of the Liturgy only a few Orthodox receive Communion, and most, if not all, of the service is sung by the clergy
and the choir or chanters. To contemporary Western Christians
that means that Orthodox worshippers do not really participate in
the Liturgy: they are passive spectators of a clericalized rite. That
is perhaps a superficial assessment, based on the assumption that
participation must always be active. But the opposite of active
need not be passive: it can be contemplative. There is a participation in worship which is contemplative rather than active, of the
kind appropriate in the Anglican tradition at a cathedral sung
Evensong. There is a contemplative quality about the Liturgy
and other Orthodox services from which Western Christians may
have something to learn. Contemporary Western worship is
sometimes so active that it can seem busy and be distracting.
Liturgical prayer is punctuated by directions to sit, stand or
kneel. The flow of the service is interrupted by announcements of

179

page, hymn and eucharistic prayer numbers. The goal intended is full congregational participation. But the result can sometimes be restless and unprayerful. Revised services provide for silence to be kept at certain moments, but it is more often indicated than prayerfully used. It may be that in a busy, activist world Christians need worship which is not busy and activist. Perhaps something of the contemplative quality of Orthodox worship could impart to Western worship a dimension it has either never had, or is in danger of losing.

For members of all Western Churches, entering an Orthodox church and taking part in the celebration of the Liturgy is an experience different from any they can have in their own tradition. It is an experience of a form of Christian worship shaped, like their own, within a particular historical and cultural setting. It is no less Christian worship. Many Christians are coming to realize that each of the different traditions within the Church of Christ has something to contribute to the whole Body, and needs what others can give. The Orthodox Church holds fast to the primacy of worship in the Christian life, and that itself is a necessary witness. It would be surprising if Western Christians could find nothing from which to learn in the way in which Orthodox Christians worship, and in particular in the heart of the Church's prayer, the Liturgy.

'Life of Christ' Symbolism in the Liturgy: Comparative Table

	Prothesis	Enarxis	First Entrance	Ascent to Throne	Epistle	Gos
Theodore of Mopsuestia						
Maximus the Confessor			First coming of Christ in the flesh, Passion and Resurrection	The Ascension of Christ	Instruction in the Christian life	The end world ar Second Coming Christ to the worl
Germanos	The sacrifice of Christ: Passion and Death	Prophetic foretelling of the Incarnation	Coming of the Son of God into the world	Completion of salvation and Ascension	Prokeimenon and Alleluia = Prophecies of the coming of Christ	Revelati God bro by Chris Bishop's blessing Gospel Second
Nicholas of Andida	The Virgin Birth and hidden life of Christ before his baptism	Prophetic foretelling of the Incarnation and the ministry of John the Baptist	Manifestation of Christ at his Baptism in the Jordan	Passage from the Law and the Old Covenant to the beginning of divine grace	The calling of the Apostles	The teac Christ
Nicholas Cabasilas	The Incarnation and early years of Christ; his Passion and Death foreshadowed	Prophetic witness to the coming of Christ: the time before the Baptist	Manifestation of Christ to the crowds at his Baptism		Manifestation of Christ in his teaching to the Apostles	Manifest of Chris teaching crowds
Symeon of Thessalonike	The Incarnation of Christ; his Passion and Death foreshadowed	The Incarnation and the work of the incarnate Word	The Resurrection and Ascension of Christ The coming of the Spirit	Christ's sitting at the right hand of the Father	Mission of the Apostles to the Gentiles	Proclam the Gos all the w

182

...issal of ...umens	Great Entrance	Placing of gifts on holy table	Anaphora	Elevation	After Communion
	Christ led away to his Passion	Christ laid in the tomb	The Resurrection of Christ from the dead		
...of those ...o the bridal ...f Christ	Revelation of the mystery of salvation hidden in God		Our future union with the spiritual powers of heaven	The union of all the faithful with God in the age to come	
	Christ proceeding to his mystical sacrifice	The burial of Christ in the tomb	The Resurrection of Christ		
	The Lord's journey to Jerusalem on Palm Sunday	The upper room made ready	The Last Supper	Christ's Crucifixion, Death and Resurrection	The Ascension of Christ and the coming of the Spirit
	Christ's journey to Jerusalem and his entry on Palm Sunday		Christ's Death, Resurrection, and Ascension	The Zeon = The coming of the Holy Spirit	
...f the world ...ation	The final coming of Christ			The elevation of Christ on the Cross	The Ascension of the Lord and the proclamation of the Gospel in all the world

Bibliography

General

The Orthodox Liturgy, English translation. London, SPCK, for the Fellowship of St Alban and St Sergius, 1939.

Brightman, F. E., *Liturgies Eastern and Western*, vol. 1, Eastern. Oxford, Clarendon Press, 1896.

Connolly, R. H., and Bishop, E., *The Liturgical Homilies of Narsai*. Texts and Studies, vol. 8, no. 1. Cambridge University Press, 1909.

Cresswell, R. H., *The Liturgy of the Eighth Book of 'The Apostolic Constitutions'*. London, SPCK, 1924.

Cross, F. L., ed., *St Cyril of Jerusalem's Lectures on the Christian Sacraments*. London, SPCK, 1951.

Kucharek, Casimir, *The Byzantine-Slav Liturgy of St John Chrysostom*. Alleluia Press, 1971.

Mateos, Juan, *La Célébration de la Parole dans la Liturgie Byzantine*. Orientalia Christiana Analecta 191. Rome, Pontifical Institute of Oriental Studies, 1971.

Paverd, Frans van de, *Zur Geschichte der Messliturgie in Antiocheia und Konstantinopel gegen Ende des Vierten Jahrhunderts*. Orientalia Christiana Analecta 187. Rome, Pontifical Institute of Oriental Studies, 1970.

Schmemann, A., *Introduction to Liturgical Theology*. London, Faith Press, 1966.

——, *The Eucharist: Sacrament of the Kingdom*. Crestwood, NY, St Vladimir's Seminary Press, 1988.

Schultz, H-J., *The Byzantine Liturgy: Symbolic Structure and Faith Expression*. E. T. Matthew, J. O'Connell. New York, Pueblo Publishing, 1986.

Taft, Robert, *The Great Entrance*. Orientalia Christiana Analecta 200. Rome, Pontifical Institute of Oriental Studies, 1975.

Taft, Robert, *The Liturgy of the Great Church: an Initial Synthesis of Structure and Interpretation on the Eve of Iconoclasm*. Dumbarton Oaks Papers 34–5, 1980–1.

Commentaries on the Liturgy

Bornert, R., *Les Commentaires Byzantines de la Divine Liturgie du VIIe au XVe Siècle*. Paris, Institut Français d'Etudes Byzantines, 1966.

Cabasilas, Nicholas, *The Divine Liturgy*. ET J. M. Hussey and P. A. McNulty. London, SPCK, 1960.

Dionysius, Pseudo-, *The Ecclesiastical Hierarchy*. In *The Complete Works of Pseudo-Dionysius*. ET Colum Luibheid. London, SPCK, 1987.

Germanos of Constantinople, *On the Divine Liturgy*. ET Paul Meyendorff. New York, St Vladimir's Seminary Press, 1984.

Maximus the Confessor, *The Church's Mystagogy*. In *Selected Writings of St Maximus the Confessor*. ET G. C. Berthold. New York, Paulist Press, 1985.

Architecture and Iconography

Grabar, A., *Christian Iconography: A Study of its Origins*. London and Henley, Routledge & Kegan Paul, 1969.

Kitzinger, E., *Byzantine Art in the Making*. London, Faber & Faber, 1977.

Krautheimer, R., *Early Christian and Byzantine Architecture*. The Pelican History of Art. London, Penguin Books, 1965.

Mathews, T. F., *The Early Churches of Constantinople: Architecture and Liturgy*. The Pennsylvania State University Press, 1971.

Music

Wellesz, E., *A History of Byzantine Music and Hymnography*. Oxford University Press, 1949.

List of Illustrations

We are grateful to Penguin Books and to the Pennsylvania State University Press, University Park, PA, for their permission to reproduce these illustrations.

Index

aer (veil) 126–7, 169
ambo 49; prayer behind 89, 122,
  138
anaphora 8; Apostolic
  Constitutions 42–4; St
  Basil 55–6; St John
  Chrysostom 56–7; silent
  recitation 86–7; Nicholas of
  Andida's understanding 142–3;
  = antidoron 139
'angel of peace' biddings 119–20
antidoron 138–9, 170
antiphons 110–12
Apostolic Constitutions 38–45
apse see sanctuary; decoration 4,
  31, 74–5, 107, 132, 149
Arianism 27–8
atrium 47–8, 72

Balsamon, Theodore 129
Barberini Codex 108
basilica 29–30, 47–9

Cabasilas, Nicholas 158;
  commentary 158–64
Cherubic Hymn 83–4
church houses 21–2
Chrysostom, John 47; interpreta-
  tion of Eucharist 61–6
church building, symbolic
  interpretation Maximus 96–7;
  Germanos 123–4; Nicholas of
  Andida 133; Symeon of
  Thessalonike 165–6
Clementine Liturgy see Apostolic
  Constitutions
Clement of Rome 14–15
Communion 36, 44, 59–60, 88–9;
  decline in lay 37;

consequences 60–1; more
  frequent 178
consecration, theology 19, 35,
  157–8
creed 84–6
Cyril of Jerusalem, Mystagogical
  Catecheses 33–8

decoration, church see
  iconography
Didascalia Apostolorum 20
Dionysius the Areopagite 90–4
diptychs 57–9
dismissals 39, 51, 81
dome 73; decoration 3, 107,
  130–1, 150–1
doxologies, trinitarian 28
Dura Europos 21–2

Ecclesiastical History see
  Germanos
eileton (corporal) 64, 126
ektene 113–14
elevation 121
Enarxis 136–8; see also antiphons
entry chant 77
entry into church 76–7;
  prayer 77
epiclesis 34–5, 43, 157–8
epitaphios 169
Eutychius, Patriarch of
  Constantinople 82

Germanos, Patriarch of
  Constantinople 108, 123–8
Great Entrance 7–8; origins 20–
  1, 52–4; development 81–3;
  prayer 116–7; interpretation:
  Germanos 126; Nicholas of

187

Index